How to Become A Wholesale Millionaire

By

Mark Lane

TABLE OF CONTENTS

How to Become a Wholesale Millionaire

How to Become a Wholesale Millionaire creator Mark Lane is a wholesaling and rehabbing expert. Although creating massive cash in real estate has made him a fortune, his real passion is teaching other people how to become fulfilled and live the life of their dreams.

Mark Lane was born in 1978 in Iowa City, Iowa to Rudy and Sharon Lane, and he still resides in Iowa today. Mark grew up middle class and continued on an average pace through life. He graduated high school with no honors and is happy to admit that school was not his "thing." Mark reluctantly went to the local community college after his mother convinced him it was his only option. Eighteen months later Mark gladly dropped out and entered the workforce full time.

Mark held a wide variety of jobs including working at restaurants, home improvement stores, lumberyards, a grocery store, and a factory. At the age of thirty he realized he would never be happy working for someone else. At the same time he was bit by the real estate bug and jumped into real estate full time. In the first year he and his partner built up over a dozen rentals. The following year, Mark flipped over twenty houses and changed the reality of his life. In the third year he continued flipping houses and began wholesaling houses on a massive scale.

In just a short time he was earning over $50,000 a month consistently from his wholesaling business with little to no work of his own. He built the same wholesaling system that he trains people on today.

Mark is a speaker, life coach, real estate investor, entrepreneur, and most importantly a role model to young people in his community. Mark is passionate about his foundation, Fathers for the Lost, a foundation focused on underprivileged kids with no father figures in their lives.

He spends every extra minute with his loving wife Rachelle and his three beautiful daughters Tiana, Ariana, and Isabelle.

Introduction

If you haven't noticed, there is a very interesting problem in our country and in our world right now, and it's getting worse by the day. It's called "everyone is broke and miserable." How often do you see someone alive with passion, energy and purpose? How often do you see people go to work loving what they do? How many people do you know who are selfsufficient, who don't depend on benefits, a job, unemployment, or Social Security? It's very, very rare. This is my purpose for writing this book and coming up with this system. I wrote this book to get it into the hands of people like yourself – people who are ready to take back their lives – and maybe I can be a part of your truly believing in yourself again. I want to do my part to show people that they do have what it takes to succeed and to live the life of their dreams. They just need some direction, and this book will be just the road map.

If you look at the Great Depression, or any of the major recessions since, you will find that during those times there has also been the largest rise in new ideas, innovations, wealth, and success. Why? My guess is because all these brilliant people like yourself realize that the only one who can truly take care of you is you. We were not created to feed off other people. We realize that this big promise that we would be secure in our jobs till retirement is simply a big lie. We realize that working our fingers to the bone twelve hours a day actually doesn't get us ahead.

People turn to themselves and a greater calling. Yes, it can be scary, but we only get to live this life once. At the end of your life are you going to be grateful that you played it safe and never took any chances? Will you be sick with regret, wondering what could've been? Who could you have helped if you would have achieved your dreams? How would it have affected your children and generations to come? How much more fun and adventurous could life have been?

The fear of not doing must be greater than the fear of *doing*! For me that meant not doing anything to advance myself would mean I would be stuck in a dead-end job for another thirty years and I never would've lived up to my God-given potential. I wouldn't have had the chance to affect other people and their families. That fear was much worse than getting uncomfortable and trying something new. How about you?

The time to dream again is *now* and the time to achieve something greater is now! Whether it be by divine purpose or by chance that you are reading this book is beyond me, but I believe with all my heart that it can and will change your life if you allow it to.

It has always been known that real estate creates more millionaires than any other industry. The main reason is because most of those involved in real estate are business owners and entrepreneurs. By entering this system you are going into business for yourself. For some that is no big deal, but for others it will be the scariest thing in your life. It's understandably scary. Most of us were never groomed to handle business on our own. Maybe we didn't have the family tree that was made up of business owners and entrepreneurs, or maybe we were just taught to play it safe, get a job, and save for retirement. Do those words ring a bell? They sure do to me. Just bear with me, and you'll see that I have everything laid out for you. I made this as foolproof as it can possibly be, because that's how I need things taught to me.

The system that you are going to learn about is real estate wholesaling on steroids. This system uses leverage to the max, so you can get maximum return for as little work and time possible.

I have been involved in real estate for many years and have had both my ups and downs. I left a factory job to become a real estate investor. In my first year I bought twelve properties using no money of my own. I didn't have a choice – I didn't have any money! My second year I flipped twenty houses. During some months I had no checks coming in, and other months I made $50,000 or more.

After a couple years of flipping houses I was in a different financial position, but I still found myself broke some months after using all my capital for expenses, paying contractors, and buying materials. But I was in real estate full time so If I didn't buy, fix, and sell a house, then I didn't get paid and my family didn't eat.

Enter wholesaling. I went to a seminar that gave me a serious wake up call! I thought I was really good doing thirty deals a year – after all, that was the most anyone in my area was doing. But some of these guys at this seminar were doing over *five hundred* deals a year, mostly wholesaling. Needless to say I was humbled and my mind was blown. I went home and got right to work figuring out a system so I could do the same thing. Three months later I made a total profit of $43,000 in a month just by wholesaling seven houses. It didn't take any money, credit, ownership, or repairs. At that point I was totally hooked and totally free.

One thing I had going for me was the knowledge I picked up from the years of being in the business. I had attended very expensive seminars and courses. I had intimate knowledge of my area and I had time to put myself out there. I'm guessing that you may be anxious right now and saying "Well crap, I don't have any of these." No worries. I built this system for someone starting from scratch. You don't have to have an ounce of knowledge to be able to work this system. All you have to do is follow the directions. It's no different than a McDonald's – all those employees have to do is follow the directions. They don't have to think, they just have to do. This will be the same, except you will have the ability to get paid as much as you want.

It's a fact that there are some people who don't finish a book they've started. Please don't let that be you. If you're picking this book up, there is a reason for it. Maybe you're unhappy at work and want to find your "thing" or your purpose. Maybe you want to be able to stay home with your kids before it's too late, or maybe you are like me and just want to make a ridiculous amount of money so you can enjoy life! Being average seems to be the "in" thing these days. I say be just the opposite. Go crazy on this! What do you have to lose? Chances are not much, and you have so much to gain. You can truly have anything you desire if you believe it and follow a proven system that is sure to get you there.

In the pages of this book I'm going to share with you both my failures and successes. You will learn about real estate and why wholesaling will always be in demand. You will also learn how to duplicate this system and how to set it up in any market throughout the country. I am going to take you step by step through each successive stage of a wholesale deal, as well as give you scripts and outlines for speaking with the team you will be building. I'm going to take all the confusion out for you. By the end I'm sure that you will see the big picture and realize how quickly you could be on your way to financial freedom.

Most of all, I hope that by the end you have an exciting new vision for your life.

Chapter 1: What Is Wholesaling?

Real estate wholesaling is matchmaking. When wholesaling, you're doing nothing more complicated than going through the steps of finding properties and matching them with cash buyers. People often overcomplicate it. There are really just a few steps to understanding how a wholesale deal is done.

You have to know how to find the deals.

You have to know how to find the buyers.

You have to know how the contracts and/or closing process works.

Obviously we're going to go into much more depth on each topic, but this is wholesaling in a nutshell... finding great undervalued properties, bringing them to your cash hungry buyers, and then closing the deals so you get paid. Although in this book we're only going to discuss the topic of wholesaling houses, you need to understand that virtually anything can be wholesaled. Many people have become filthy rich by wholesaling. eBay is wholesaling. Craigslist is wholesaling. Walmart is wholesaling.

You can wholesale apartment buildings, vacant lots, houses, cars, clothes, etc. Look at all the consignment shops that are going up... this is wholesaling... buying low from one person then marking it up slightly so you can make a profit, but sell it right away. That is wholesaling. I sincerely hope you understand the simplicity of it. Once you understand how simple it is, it will be that much easier for you.

Why Wholesaling?

There are a number of reasons why people get into wholesaling and stay there aside from flipping houses, holding rentals, selling houses on contract, etc. For me it really came down to the speed of money, no stress, and the ROI (return on investment) and ROT (return on time). Unlike How to rehabbing houses, wholesaling is done without using any money. You don't have to worry about a credit score, don't have to worry about banks, doesn't take much time, and it can be set up as a system better than rehabbing.

When a person decides they want to flip a house, they generally spend hours looking at houses before they ever offer on one. Once they offer, they still have to inspect it, get estimates from their contractor, and find or decide on financing. Then once all that is done and the house has been purchased, there is a walk through with the contractor, picking out materials, and check ups each week to make sure work is being done. Once it's completed, then comes time to list it, deal with negotiations, inspections on the buyer's side, more repairs, and finally a hopefully smooth closing. I speak from experience – I have rehabbed hundreds of houses.

With wholesaling, the deal generally takes all of four hours or less. I tell people the best way to look at it is how many wholesales could you do in the amount of time it takes you to do one rehab project? I'm not saying don't ever rehab a house, but be very selective. My recommendation is to not rehab a house unless you will make $30,000 or more. If you're going to rehab and you are planning for a $20,000 profit, there is a good chance that costs will go over, the closing will take longer, etc., and you'll be down to a $15,000 profit or less. In that time you may have been able to do ten wholesale deals averaging $5,000 each. It just makes sense when you look at it from this point of view.

With wholesaling, you have a more consistent flow of paychecks, also known as "speed of money." One reason rehabbers often don't get ahead is because they are waiting months between paychecks. If you are like most people, then you know that expenses add up quickly, especially when there is no income coming in. I have been in this position many times...using what capital I had to invest into my rehabs, waiting two to three months for a sale, then getting a big paycheck and having to use it all to pay off all my late bills. This adds up to nothing more than a big ball of stress.

With wholesaling and my system, you are in complete control. If you don't have enough paychecks coming in, then you go out and build up another area, get more offers out, and get more paychecks coming in.

Even after all the wholesaling I have done, I am still amazed at how easy it really is. In fact I still get all giddy after I close a $10,000 wholesale deal that has taken me an hour or two. Where else can you have no education, no experience, no money, and be able to go out and generate that kind of income?

Why Wholesaling Works

First off, I'm not teaching you how to be a real estate investor. In fact, wholesaling is more of an income generating business than it's a real estate strategy. You will begin to understand a lot about real estate once you get going, but you don't have to know anything to get started.

Wholesaling works in both an up and down market. The reason it works so well is that the biggest problem for most investors is finding enough good quality deals. They have their select type of property that they like to buy, and unfortunately there often isn't enough of those to go around for each investor, and so they only end up buying a fraction of what they would like to.

As a wholesaler you are catering to all your buyers and so it drastically opens up your capabilities to make a profit. Picture yourself having hundreds of cash hungry buyers… some wanting three-bed ranches, some wanting two-bed rentals, some wanting nice quality suburban homes, some wanting inner city rentals, some wanting transitional areas, some wanting town-homes or condos, some wanting small multi-units. You can see how this opens up your profit capabilities. Imagine yourself being the one finding all these excellent deals. You're no longer limited to finding one specific property. Now imagine having this system going in several cities at once, doing up to ten deals per city, per month, and making $2,500-$5,000 per deal.

The Time Is Now

In a down market you have a surplus of discounted properties, which makes finding them much easier. You also have investors who desperately want to buy up whatever they can because they know when the market turns around, their properties will increase in value.

In a hot market you have less inventory, but your buyers are even more desperate because the market is dry for them too, leading them to pay higher prices for your wholesale deals.

Whether it's a red hot market or a recession, wholesaling will always be in demand because great deals will always be in demand. The person that knows how to find these great deals will always be in demand and get paid very well for this unique skill!

As of the writing of this book, the current real estate market is on a steep climb up and it's just getting started, meaning there is another six to ten years to ride the wave. There will still be plenty of opportunity afterwards, but this unique market we are in will make the wholesalers who know what they are doing wealthy beyond belief. It's a unique market because everyone and their brother are diving into real estate. The media is starting to roar about it, which is going to create even more of a craze. Prices are going up rapidly, allowing for a higher wholesale profit; and with the surplus of hungry cash buyers flooding the market, there is increased demand for your deals.

Also, technology has made real estate investing, particularly wholesaling, easier than ever. A decade or two ago you couldn't find real estate agents, attorneys, properties, value of properties, etc. on the other side of the country. Now, from the comfort of your computer, you can! And it's ridiculously easy. Technology has allowed the system I have built to not only be possible, but to be almost automatic.

Stop Carrying Buckets

The essence of a true business owner is that instead of working in the business, like an employee does, they work *on* the business.

Here's a story that illustrates this distinction.

There was a small island in the Pacific Ocean. For their fresh water, the natives were dependent upon the well in the center of their village. One day the well suddenly ran dry. The village leaders called an emergency meeting to discuss what to do about it. After a long debate, they accepted two offers on solving this problem, with the agreement that they would pay twenty-five cents per gallon of water delivered.

The first person promised to deliver water immediately. He began hauling two buckets of water back and forth from a nearby lake to the well. He made money immediately, and he stayed very busy all day, hauling water in his buckets.

The other person also promised to deliver water, but she explained that it would take six months. She hired a contractor to construct a pump and a pipeline from the lake to the well. After six months of building the pipeline, which included a meter to measure the number of gallons coming through the pipeline, she had the pump turned on. Now she could rest and relax, and collect her residual income the rest of her life.

The point of this story is that the ideal business is one that will create for you and your family a *financial pipeline of passive income* that could last for the rest of your life. We call this residual income. This is where you have real freedom – the freedom to do what you really want with your life.

Would you agree that most people are carrying buckets, trading time for money, and are not very free? We teach people how to build a financial pipeline so that they can be free to do what they really want with their life. Does that make sense to you?

The average real estate speculator spends their time driving around neighborhoods looking for vacant houses. They send out postcards, mailers, etc. It's all very time consuming, and they get only a fraction of deals accepted that are possible with my system.

The bad news for most speculators is that they are carrying buckets, all day every day. They may still make a significant income, but they can't spend the day with their kids anytime they want, they can't take a month off, and they can't literally sit back and watch the checks pour in.

Factory Wholesaling (The Vision)

It's said that the most wealth and success is created when two industries collide. Everyone knows Henry Ford for his creation of the Ford Motor Company. Ford believed in creating a system for churning out as many cars in as little time as possible as efficiently as possible. The others in the auto business condemned him and hated him for being so awesome. Of course they did – he put all of them to shame, and most of them out of business.

Well, I am nowhere near smart enough to build a factory, nor do I want to spend my life doing so. But I do love wholesaling, and I had the vision of setting up a factory-like system of wholesaling all across the country, in every major city of every state.

Because of technology, putting this system in place is now possible. You can now have as many offers going out as you want at any given time, which will result in more deals and inevitably more checks in the mail.

Market Domination

It's almost inevitable that you will dominate any market you enter. The system is set up that way. The investors in each market you enter will be at your feet and asking for you to bring them more killer deals.

In this new era of systems, leverage, and speed of business, the person who is utilizing these will certainly dominate.

Experienced real estate investors will always have opportunity because they know how to find it. But their ways of going about it are much too slow for me. I would say that the average investor only does approximately six deals per year with an average profit of $15,000 to $20,000. That may seem great to the average person and it's a good income, but with my system that can be possible *per month*.

The old ways of real estate are becoming extinct. Leverage and systems are taking over. I once heard an investor say, "The slow way to get rich is to invest in your area." What he meant is, you can still become rich by doing deals in your area just like all the other investors are – it's just going to take a long time. But if you want to skyrocket your income, you need to spread out and have deals going on in many places.

My Two-Minute Story

My journey that led me to this system was not easy, by any means. I started in real estate by building a rental portfolio with a partner, nearly went bankrupt, killed the partnership, and sold out of all the rentals. Then I started flipping houses, worked crazy hours trying to get them all finished and on the market before my hard money loans ate up all my profit. I made a lot of money compared to anything I had made in the past. I paid off all my bad debt, spent a lot of money, and found myself broke again! The next year I flipped even more houses, tripled my income and still found myself broke at the end of the year... and exhausted. By my fourth year I was a little wiser, paid for some really expensive mentoring, had my "ah hah" moment, actually saved my money, and began wholesaling on a regular basis. Within just a few months I was averaging over $50,000 a month! And I was still only doing deals in my city.

I didn't have to worry about managing rehab projects, managing rentals, insurance, utilities, or lenders. Wholesaling became a way to achieve the income I desired without all the stress.

Shortly after I was making up to $10,000 on what seemed like a daily basis, I thought about what it would take to expand it on a larger scale. At the same time I had numerous people asking me to coach them on how I did this. Essentially, what my success led to is a higher calling of wanting to help people like you instead of helping only myself. It led me to an amazing vision and book, and here we are.

Chapter 2: My Sucky Life

I really shouldn't title this chapter "My Sucky Life," because the fact is that due to my loving and supporting parents I had a wonderful childhood. I have a wonderful family, have always been healthy, and have really only struggled financially – but as a man, that can sometimes feel like carrying a mountain.

Nearly all of my life I've been middle class. There's the saying that goes "You don't know what you don't know." Well, I didn't know any different, and to my knowledge neither did my parents. I didn't have any direction in my life when it came to creating a higher income. My mom tried forcing me into college, which she was successful at, but only for a bit over a year. Within a short time I had had enough. I couldn't stand it, and maybe it shows by my writing style. Language and creative writing were not my strong suit. I would have rather stabbed myself in the eye with a fork than have stayed in school – it just wasn't for me. After dropping out of community college I went into the workforce full time. I tried out a couple different trades, worked at restaurants, worked as a personal trainer, lumber yards, home improvement stores... you name it and there is a good chance I did something close to it.

In my young twenties I found myself without a driver's license after passing a state patrol car going 110 mph on my crotch rocket. I really don't advise that. The losing your license part really blows. I had to find a job within walking distance of my dad's apartment – oh yeah, I forgot to mention the part about my girlfriend dumping me cause I was now jobless, sleeping in till noon, and having no purpose. It was obvious that success was not knocking on my door. The job I got while staying with my dad was at a grocery store within walking distance.

I worked at the grocery store and after just a couple months I was promoted to frozen food manager. Now I was moving up in the world! I had a black nametag and was making $28,000 a year. That's a joke by the way – name tags mean someone owns you. After a few more months I was promoted again to assistant manager at $32,000 a year. It wasn't much but it was the most I had ever made, so I thought maybe I ought to give this place some consideration for longer employment.

After another promotion I was third in charge of the store, but was now working sixty hours a week for a measly $36,000 a year. I had the goals and was in training for the store director position, which at that time could pay anywhere between $80,000 and $150,000. After three more years of working sixty hours a week and getting turned down for numerous promotions, I started getting the feeling that I was at a dead end. I had to ask myself, "If I ever make it to that position, how long will it take and will the time spent to achieve it be worth it?"

My answer resulted in my two-week notice shortly after.

I left that "job" for another. This time it was a completely new industry to me... a factory. The idea of getting paid overtime for all my extra hours sounded great, as I had been on salary for the past five years.

The first six months were kind of fun because I got to learn something new for a change, but after the newness wore off I found myself more miserable than ever. For much of my time at the factory I was working up to twelve-hour nights. I had never worked a graveyard shift before and I can honestly say it was torture. At one point we were even getting asked to work sixteen-hour days. I remember countless times pulling in the driveway after a full day and wondering how I even got home. It was only a matter of time before I fell asleep at the wheel or hung myself from one of the overhead tracks.

The thoughts of working another thirty years there haunted me day and night, and each day it got worse. I was turning into a zombie, my health went downhill and no matter how much overtime I worked there was never anything to show for it as taxes were eating it all up.

One night in particular I remember coming home from a night shift. I walked in, put my stuff down, and made my way up to the bedroom. My daughter, who was about two years old at the time, lay there asleep with my wife, stress-free and not a worry in the world. She had no idea of the personal hell I was going through every day. As I lay down next to her I began to weep, not for myself, but for the example that I was setting for her. I didn't want her to grow up to be average. I didn't want her to grow up without a purpose. I didn't want her to grow up struggling to pay bills each month. Most of all I wanted her to grow up to be strong, confident, and successful because she learned from me setting an example.

That night in my midst of weeping I made a vow to her that I would change, that I would become someone of significance, that I would be able to provide above and beyond anything she'd ever need. I made the vow to be a leader to my household, and I knew that in order to keep this vow I would have to find a solution and a purpose.

Thank God for Infomercials

Shortly after the vow to my daughter I found myself staring at young guy on TV at 4:00 am talking about real estate and trying to sell me a book. I'd always been impressed by businessmen and always wanted to flip a house, so I thought, "What the heck do I have to lose?" Days later I was through the book, cover to cover. Then I bought another, and another, and another. The more I read the more I started to feel empowered. I started to get that feeling like "Yeah, I think I can do this." Keep in mind I was still at the factory, but I was reading every chance I got... during breaks, lunches, during the drive home (don't do that). Every chance I had I was soaking it up. I was acting successful and didn't even realize it. Successful people do what most people won't do!

After a short time I ventured out and started trying to put this stuff to work to see what would happen. I was hanging signs, calling real estate agents, calling banks, calling attorneys, basically I was building my team like the books had taught me to. After a couple months of getting nowhere I hung up my real estate career, put my head down, and went back to work every day, but at least this time I had a new vision for my life. I knew I wasn't going to be a factory worker for the rest of my life–I just had to find the vehicle to get me out of there.

The next summer my wife and I were having a garage sale. We were trying to make extra money by selling what we could since I had been laid off and lost a large portion of my income. One of the boxes I opened had the first few real estate books that I had read. Something told me to go through them again. I did, and again I felt more empowered.

A short time later I went to a free real estate seminar. It was really just to pump us up so we would buy into their upcoming three-day seminar. It cost $500 to go to the three-day seminar. I hurried to the back of the room to slap down my credit card. I just knew I had to go. I was beyond excited and I called my wife to tell her. To say she didn't agree would be an understatement! She still had the mindset that all this stuff was a big scam. I can say that freely because now she knows otherwise!

During the three-day seminar my mind was totally blown. I had never been to anything like that before, but I was in love. Hundreds of people gathered there for the same purpose–to enrich their life.

But during the second day I started to get the feeling that we were being sold on yet another package. This time it was into the tens of thousands. Obviously I didn't have the money for that, so I sat there frustrated and dejected while I saw numerous people walking around with their big black bags of goodies that came with packages they had purchased. My heart was pounding, my throat was on fire, and my eyes were burning... I don't know

23

if it was anger, passion, jealousy or what, all I knew is that I wanted more and I wasn't going to stop until real estate was a part of my life.

After going home empty-handed but hope-filled, I got right to work. I hit the streets and put everything I had learned to use. One of the guys from the seminar with whom I stayed in contact surprised me one day when he asked if I'd like to partner with him on the package he purchased from the seminar. I didn't know what to think. I believe the good Lord had some divine appointments set up that day.

Within just a couple months we had purchased our first rental home. The next month another, and the next month another. My work ethic coupled with his great job and credit allowed us the opportunity to buy, fix, and rent these homes. Then we would refinance and do it all over again. Within just over a year I believe we had purchased a dozen rentals.

Although I was on cloud nine because I was doing what I most desired, I was also still broke. After the third house we bought I quit my job so I could focus on real estate full time. I had no income and we were making peanuts for cash flow from the properties.

Into the second year I had also flipped three houses and very quickly realized that the influx of cash did a lot for relieving the stress at home. Within a short time I decided to dissolve the partnership. I was growing as an investor from all my day-to-day action while my partner still had a nine-to-five job. It just got to the point where it didn't make sense to have a partner anymore.

The next year I went crazy, flipping twenty houses. Life was getting better and I loved what I was doing. I had tripled my income at this point, but things were still stressful. Expenses were rising, with new cars, private school for the kids, eating out, and more frequent trips, coupled with managing dozens of houses under construction and handling hundreds of thousands of dollars per transactions.

Some months I would make a killing, and then I might go three or four months without a paycheck. Rising expenses would eat up all the profit I previously made. It always seemed like I was broke every few months or so. This continued up to the day that I learned how to wholesale.

How I Turned $10,000 into $50,000

I got invited out to another real estate seminar – free of charge this time, due to my success story. During that amazing two-day weekend we were given the option to sign up for more advanced training, given through yet another three-day course. Yes, I bought into it! Success minded people don't think about the cost; we only think about what it will do for us and what it will make us in return. During that course I was blown away yet again. It was far more advanced than anything else I had gone through up to that point.

This course was really centered around wholesaling. Although I got well more than my money's worth there were still some things left out that I had to figure out on my own. So as soon as I got back to town I hit the streets, this time differently than before. I was making far more offers, working less, and getting more houses accepted. In essence I was trying to build that pipeline.

A few times I almost got myself in trouble. I was buying so many houses I was scrambling to come up with the money to close them all. Although I was trying to wholesale, I was still in the habit of buying and holding or buying and flipping.

With wholesaling you never even buy. You just get a property under contract at a great price then immediately find a buyer who wants to buy it, and you sign the contract over to him for compensation. You get paid just for finding properties that match what your buyers are looking for.

After constantly tweaking my system and much help from my real estate agent and attorney, I was able to develop a nearly hands-off wholesaling system that is active today. In fact, three months after the weekend training I had made over $50,000 in a month just from wholesaling... and it's getting better by the day.

Proof That It Works

Below are samples of some checks that come in on almost a daily basis. I still enjoy flipping houses, but wholesaling is a skill that when done correctly can make you rich in a hurry. There is no stress to it, and once you get this system set up correctly you will be on your way to freedom! You can grow this as big as you want to. How much you make will finally be up to you, and not your boss or the economy. Remember, this is all about setting up the pipeline so you have constant deal flow leading to constant check cashing. Once you start to have $2,500 to $10,000 worth of checks being sent to you by mail on almost a daily basis, you'll realize that life has forever changed and you will hopefully be sending me a giant thank you.

Enjoy salivating over these!

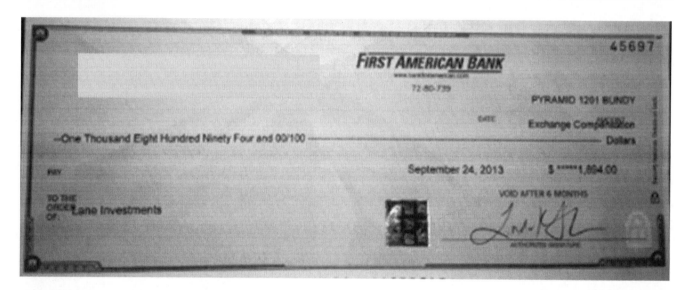

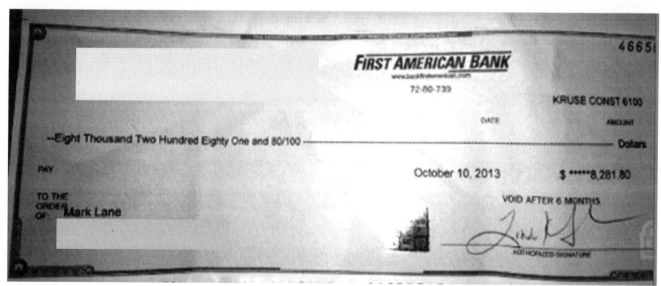

Keep in mind that I have checks like these showing up in my mailbox is now almost a daily occurrence. Everything I do is in these pages. Most people never have the opportunity to cash $7,500 and $10,000 checks. If you follow what I have outlined, this will be a reality for you too.

What will your life be like if this were a daily or weekly occurrence for you? Or let's say you don't have the same results, but you do one a month. An extra $5,000 to $10,000 a month for most people would be life changing. It would allow breathing room, maybe a dream vacation, a new car, or savings for the kids' college. What you use it for is totally up to you, but it will not happen without following the steps outlined within this book.

Chapter 3: An Overview

In this chapter we'll be going through a brief summary of each step of a wholesale deal and how this system is approached. What you learn here is going to be far different than what you will learn in any other wholesaling course. Why? Because we're going to be setting it up as a pipeline so the deals are constantly coming to you. You will not be doing all the other time consuming things all the other wholesalers are doing. The point here is to leverage each step so that you're getting maximum efficiency and doing as little as possible, and therefore building up more markets for more deals.

Area of Choice – The coolest thing about this system is that it will work exactly the same anywhere in the country. Results will differ from area to area, but the framework of the system will be the same anywhere. You're going to learn exactly how to quickly find a market, its population, its potential, and more. This will all be done from the comfort of your computer or smart phone.

"A" Players – In order to leverage this system you absolutely must have A Players on your team. That means professionals on your team that you never have to worry about. I have hired and fired more people than you could shake a stick at. And after firing each one of them I instantly have less stress because there is no more babysitting. You don't have time for babysitting–you're going to be building an extremely profitable wholesaling business and it must be centered around the right people.

Real Estate Agents – Your real estate agents are going to be the blood of your business. Without them your wholesaling business will not succeed. Eighty percent of the deals you will ever do are going to be on market deals, meaning listed on the MLS. So without an A Player real estate agent, you cannot and will not succeed. You're going to learn exactly how to find one, the scripts to use to screen them, and how to quickly see if they are going to be right for this system. I'm even going to show you a trick on how to have the best agents in any market found for you.

Attorneys/Title Companies – These are the professionals who are going to be doing your closings. A wholesale deal is not closed like a traditional closing; therefore you will need a professional in this field who knows how to properly close one of these deals.

Buyers – Wholesaling is centered around your buyers. Without your buyers you won't have anyone to take your deals to. You will learn how to find hundreds of buyers within a day or two. I will show you how to instantly find a whole list of buyers off Craigslist by a simple search. Also, how to effectively market so your buyers are calling and begging to be on your list.

The Offering System – Every real estate investor I know who is #1 in his market got that way because of the amount of offers he makes, resulting in the amount of deals he gets, and further resulting in the amount of checks he cashes. With this system you will have an offer on every single foreclosure, short sale, estate, and motivated seller property on the market. And best of all, you will never have to write an offer again! If you haven't been in this business long then you have no idea how valuable that is. Along with this system you'll see the spreadsheets of your offers and will be able to look them up whenever you want from wherever you want so you can always see the status. When you're done with this part you'll see and understand exactly why this system works and how it's approached as a numbers game. There is never any guesswork.

Your Deal Package – If you're doing one deal at a time you can easily make a phone call or two to your investors and likely have it sold if it's a good deal. But what do you do when you have numerous deals a week or month coming in? You need to have a presentation process for this. You will learn how to put this package together, and more importantly how to leverage your real estate agent to do most of this for you. This package will include pictures of your property, a CMA (comparative market analysis), an estimated profit and/ or cash flow, and ROI (return on investment). Don't be intimidated by the terminology– your agent will do all the hard work for you, all you will have to do is punch some numbers into a spreadsheet and hit send.

Closing the Deal – This goes along with your attorney or closing agent, but I want to give just a little more focus here so you will be comfortable seeing your deal through to closing. After all, this is where you get paid, so it's important to have your ducks in a row. You will even know how to set your system up for this so that your attorney knows exactly what to do for your deals.

Overcoming Obstacles

It's a universal law that life can be tough and new things are scary. I believe it's set up this way so that those who are willing to face the challenge, to step it up, to get uncomfortable for awhile will also receive the greatest rewards. If taking a risk were easy, everyone would do it. But it's not. It's scary and uncomfortable. This is why I laid everything out in a way that all you really have to do is follow directions, follow the scripts, and pick up your checks–or better yet have them mailed to you. The sad part is no matter how easy I make this, there will still only be a very small percentage of people who will actually do it. Let's quickly discuss what obstacles people most often have that keep them from success and wholesaling riches, and how to overcome them.

Mindset

A person's thought pattern is ultimately what is responsible for where they end up in life. I often find myself wondering what goes through the mind of a sixty-year-old man who's sitting on the street corner with a cigarette in his mouth. I'm not judging here, but his thoughts led him to his destination. At the same time the thirty-year-old millionaire with a solid family and lots of freedom is where he's at due to his thought pattern.

Some people are groomed to have a strong mindset. They are encouraged, loved, nurtured, and mentored, and have consequently developed a strong mind. Others are beat down, treated poorly, groomed for poverty, and therefore have confidence issues, believe they're not good enough to succeed, believe money is not easy to make, and end up struggling their whole life. It's sad but it's truth.

However, no matter where you and your mindset are at right now, understand that it can change! Start taking responsibility for you and your actions! We as a nation and a whole need to do this. You may have had a rough life or a good life, but you are the only one who can make your life better, so you have to start having a mindset of abundance. You have to start believing in yourself and your new purpose. If you want this to work, then you have to believe that it works. Above all else, your mindset is your starting point.

Time

Time may be the second most limiting factor. I totally get it. I have a wife, three kids, I work out, have a thriving business, kids activities, help in the community, have meetings, etc. Life is darn busy, but it's no reason to not chase your dreams. In fact it may be even more of a reason. If you make this work for you and create the life of your dreams, do you think you can enjoy yourself more in everything you do? Will you enjoy family time more by being able to do the things you never thought possible? Will you enjoy your days and nights more when you don't have to think about going to a job anymore? I can tell you that the peace of not having to wake up to an alarm is one of the best feelings of all.

All self-made successful people know and understand the meaning of delayed gratification and/or sacrifice. It means you may have to sacrifice something now to gain something later. In this instance we are talking about time.

When I worked at the factory, by most peoples' standards I didn't have any extra time. But I knew that I had to make time. I had to squeeze it out of somewhere. Much of this system can be done in an hour or two per day. Do you have that much extra time in your day? I don't know you, but I can guarantee you do. The average American watches four hours of TV per night. You could cut out an hour of sleep, work through your lunch breaks to get off work earlier, or work on this during your lunch break. You could organize your errands so they are all done on one day or at the same time. These are just a few ideas, but I think you get the point. Time is by far our most precious commodity. We waste so much of it. Start putting your time into something that is going to pay you back.

Takes Too Much Time

Wholesaling can be time consuming. But with this system it's nearly all leveraged for you. It's set up to maximize your time, outsource to others yet be in control the whole time. The income that will be produced from this when weighed out at an hourly rate should equal in the thousands of dollars per hour. Take that to the bank... and I mean that literally.

Not Enough Deals

As I said before, eighty percent of the deals you ever get will be on market deals, and we will be leveraging the MLS to its maximum potential. There are more deals to be had than you will ever be able to do, period! The reason that holds true is because you can easily have this system going in a few markets at the same time. You will also learn how to pull deals from two other sources. The reason many wholesalers aren't doing enough deals is because they are not using the MLS to their advantage and making enough offers. The more offers you make, the more deals you will get. It's a numbers game.

Can't Get the Deals Low Enough

With this system you will quickly learn how to find the bottom of your market and how to find the deals at that price and you will learn how much to mark up your deals so they are still attractive to your buyers. Getting the deals low enough to be able to make a profit comes from 1) Repetition... continuously submitting the same offer week after week, and 2) Submitting offers on the properties that are likely to accept a low offer.

Don't Profit Enough from Wholesaling

If you're not profiting enough from wholesaling, then there are two things you are doing wrong. 1) Not getting the deals cheap enough, and 2) Not marketing to your buyers well. Starting out, you need to determine what the minimum profit is you will take on a deal. $500? $1,000? $2,500? I won't do a deal unless I can make $2,500... because at this point, it's just not worth my time when I can focus on deals that will make me more. I had a girl at a seminar say to me, "I hope I never get to the point where I won't do a deal for $500." I said, "Why don't you just repeat that to yourself and see how that sounds?" She was trying to be humble and keep things in perspective, but as we grow our perspective and what we will settle for needs to change with it. Why would you not want to get to that point? The better you get at this the more your time will be worth. My average wholesale deal at this point nets me approximately $8,000 and generally takes me less than an hour. I am constantly working on efficiency and better deals so that average deal gets better and better and you should too.

Can't Get Your Real Estate Agent to Make Enough Offers

If you run into this problem, then you simply don't have an A Player real estate agent. If you have an A Player on your team they will find a way to get it done. If you find yourself babysitting them and having to constantly ask them how many offers are being made then move on *immediately*. They are the most important part of your team, so having the right one is a must. You may have to go through a dozen or more until you find the right one, but when you do you will know. You will have proof by being able to look at your spreadsheet!

<u>NOT A BIG ENOUGH WHY</u>

I capitalized and underlined this for a reason. You need to understand its importance and how it will affect your results. If you don't have a big enough "why," it's almost guaranteed that you won't keep going. Some obstacle will be big enough to slow you down, and once you slow down you will eventually stop. If you do have a big enough why, then you will have a purpose deep enough to make it through anything, and that is a purpose worth searching for. Maybe you know right now what your why is, or maybe you need to do some soul searching. When you find it I recommend you write it down and keep it with you at all times in a wallet, purse or whatever it takes so you won't lose it. This needs to be more valuable to you than anything.

My purpose is my daughters' future. Not so much financially, but more so their confidence and belief in themselves. I want them to know that beyond any doubt that when they puts their minds to something that they will achieve it. As they grow up I want them to know that the person who is closest to them made it happen in their lives, so it will be common ground for them to believe that as truth.

Here are some questions to get you thinking. Be patient; it may take some time to discover it, but when you do it should also get you choked up because it's usually kept back in the deep dark part of our souls that we don't visit very often.

Who am I doing this for?

Why am I committing to this?

How is this going to change my future?

How is this going to change my family's future?

How will this make me happier?

How will I be able to help others by becoming successful?

After you answer each question, take it a few levels deep by continuing to ask "why?"

For example:

How is this going to change my family's future?

Answer: It will give them the confidence to know they can do whatever they believe in.

Why?

Because I will have led the way and proved that we can change and reach whatever we focus on.

Why?

Because I love them and want to give them everything.

Why?

Because they are my life and I don't want them to feel insecure like I did.

Why?

Because it hurts and is humiliating and I don't want them to go through that.

As you can see, with just a few sets of "why" we quickly get to the root of why we want or need to do this, and it usually ends with wanting to avoid pain or wanting our loved ones to avoid it.

We went through a lot of obstacles that you may end up facing, but you can do this! It's a system! It's not something that you are going to have to go out and try on your own and fail and try something else. Take comfort in knowing that. I failed enough for both of us, and that's how I was able to come up with this.

Have faith in yourself, in this system, be persistent, and let it work for you!

Now let's get into the nuts and bolts of this system and exactly how it works.

Chapter 4: Working With A Players

Every extremely successful person knows and understands the importance of working with A Players. An A Player is the best of the best, the cream of the crop, the alpha male or female. These people are generally born this way. It's in their genetics to be great and to do more than others. God created these people to get a lot of stuff done!

Why is it so important to find these people? Because you are going to be leveraging this system to the max and you need to have people who are going to be able to get the job done without having to be babysat the whole time. In each area of this process you will need to find these people, and I will show you exactly how to do it. I've had several real estate agents during my career, and with this story you'll be able to see the difference in their mentality and how they handle things.

When I first started getting into wholesaling full time, I had one real estate agent with whom I was doing almost all my business. We'll call him agent A. He specialized in foreclosures, so he shouldn't have had a problem writing low offers, but apparently he did. We wrote an offer on an estate sale. It was listed for $80,000 and we wrote the offer for $51,106, and a couple days later I got it accepted with no counter offer at all. The listing agent for the seller sent agent A an email needing a bit of information. Mistakenly, agent A forwarded that email to me, and he must have forgotten about the email he sent to the listing agent when he offered on the property. In short, he *apologized* to the listing agent for writing such a low offer, and even went so far as to say, "I'm sure we won't make a deal here." Because of his mindset, he was embarrassed to write such offers, and he didn't believe this kind of stuff worked. Hopefully he learned his lesson when I did seven deals that month for a total of over $50,000 in profit.

During my third year of real estate I started working with another real estate agent who specialized in short sales. We will call him agent B. Agent B was incredibly motivated and his business showed it. He was continuously winning awards, was increasing his sales consistently, was president of his local Chamber of Commerce, was always ahead of the game with technology, and had a family to spend time with. One day a conversation started over wholesaling and agent B made a remark about it, but it was a positive remark. It was something along the likes of, "I've been to all the investment seminars just like you have, and I know how it works."

After a week, agent B and I sat down for lunch and spoke about how we could do more deals and do it more efficiently. It was the birthplace of this system! In fact, he was the one who helped create the offering system. In his mind he thought, well if I write more offers and do more deals then not only will it help this investor, but it will increase my sales even more. He even said, "Well, if it takes too much time then I will have to hire someone to take care of it."

Most other agents will have the poor mentality and say it takes too much time. They are not A Players. Or they will say it doesn't work. They are not A Players. Maybe they will say you can't find deals that low in your market. They are not A Players.

You will need to find A Players for every contact you have to make. It's important to note that many people can seem like an A Player at first and then prove themselves to be otherwise. When you do get rid of them, get on the phone and find another one. There is no need to settle for people that aren't going to help your business grow. You need to be doing business with the people who want to make your business grow, as in turn it will help theirs.

Find people with the "how can I" attitude.

Chapter 5: How to Find a Target Market

Step 1

You might be thinking that you need to start in your own backyard, in your city. Almost any real estate course teaches you to start in your area. I say think and act differently. The new realm of possibilities is doing everything virtually. You can go faster, do more, and be more efficient doing real estate this way. In fact it may be very self-defeating to limit yourself to your area. If you live in a small town with a population of 2,500, then you will not be able to make this system work for you in your market. Instead, feel free to start in any market you choose. Below are three ways in determining an optimum market. You can implement this process in as many markets as you like until you choose one that feels good.

Population – Having a small population can certainly ruin your chances of having enough wholesale deals coming through the pipeline. Having too large of population leads to more opportunity, but it can also lead to confusion and more work. I recommend starting with a city with a minimum population of 150,000 and preferably in the 250,000 to 350,000 range. This range will give you ample properties to have offers on and keep your real estate agent working hard but not getting burned out. Cities with this size population also have enough investors to buy from you. It doesn't do you any good if you get a couple properties locked up and you can't find any investors to move them to.

How to Find City Population

On Google, search for your state of choice plus cities by population. For example... "Iowa cities by population." The first search to show up for almost every state is Wikipedia. If you choose a state and it doesn't show up, then one of the other top five searches will provide you with nearly the same thing. Next, click on the Wikipedia link, and it should automatically pull up exactly what you are looking for. Usually it will pull up the search with the cities with highest population at top and works its way down. If it doesn't, then scroll over to the population tab and click the up/down arrow so that highest population is at the top. So for Iowa, the largest city is Des Moines at 206,688, and next it's Cedar

Rapids with 128,119. Keep in mind that many of these cities will have suburbs that will make up the metro area. The Des Moines metro population is roughly 588,000. Once you find a city that has roughly what you are looking for, you can Google "your city, state" plus "metro population." The metro areas are almost always included on the MLS of the city you want to work in so you don't need to worry about setting up business in all these suburbs.

So whatever state or city you might have an interest in, you can find out its population from just a few clicks at your computer.

Listings on the Market – It's important to have enough listings on the market you are going to be working in. Having a large enough population doesn't always mean everything. If by chance you are in a really hot market, you might have a good population, but you might have almost nothing on the market. In these cases everyone's property values are going up so fast that they don't sell. In these markets it's still possible to wholesale, but the chances of finding these undervalued properties is going to be rare.

How to Find Listings on the Market

For this search we will go to realtor.com. Enter your city and state of choice based off your Wikipedia search. In this search you will also need to add prices, beds, and baths. I generally do a search for prices between $25,000 and $85,000. The reason for this is that it's a price range that appeals to investors. Not every investor is filthy rich, and in fact most of them are not, so they need to be active in a price range that fits what they can handle. Also in this price range you are likely to find your undervalued starter homes or your rental homes. These are the types of properties you will be searching for to bring to your investors. For beds click on 3+, and for baths 1+. Many investors will buy two-bed homes and sometimes one-bed homes if the price is right, but on average most of them like to buy three-beds or more. Reason being is they command a higher rental price, and many investors follow the philosophy of don't buy what you won't be able to sell later.

Remember, this is just a search to see what kind of activity there is in the market you're looking at. Once you have your city, state, price, beds and baths in place, hit enter and see what happens. In Des Moines, Iowa there were 128 properties available. If I entered a different city such as Atlanta, Georgia with the same criteria I got a whopping 921. So is there more opportunity in Atlanta than there is in Des Moines? Yes – and likely many more hungry investors.

Household Median Income - Why do we need to know this? Well it's third on the list because it doesn't matter as much, but it does give you an idea of the city and the people that populate it, as well as where the city is headed. Obviously, a city where the median income is higher or going up is a city where things are happening. You don't want to do business in a market where nothing is going on. Money can be made in those markets, but it's for investors that have years to wait until those markets turn around. We are going for speed, so the more action the better.

How to Find Median Income

Again go to Google and search your city, state, and median income. For example, "Des Moines Iowa median income." The first search to pull up should be city-data.com. In a city where the median income is very low, there's likely a lot of crime and not enough good starter-type of houses on the market. In a city where the median income is extremely high it's unlikely that there are enough distressed properties. These areas have the money to keep things sharp and the residents are generally better with their money and therefore fewer foreclosures, short sales, etc. Right now in the United State the median household income is approximately $58,000, so you may want to find an area with a median income of +/- 20% of that.

However, please keep in mind that with wholesaling it's all about servicing your buyers and bringing them deals that they want. And there are investors in every area of the country. When you can find them you can literally make money anywhere! Start to think of this as a skill that you are going to own. There are so few people that are able to go into any market and generate income like you will be able to with this system.

So now you have the ability to find out vital information about any market of any city in the country... all from a few clicks of a computer... pretty sweet, huh!

Chapter 6: How to Find a Real Estate Agent

Step 2

Your real estate agent is by far the most crucial part of your wholesaling business. They will either consume your time or they will enable you to do many deals, all depending on how good they are. It's absolutely crucial that you find an agent that has a mentality for abundance. Don't expect to find an A Player real estate agent on your first call–it's highly unlikely. You should call and interview at least five. You may find one or two out of that five or you may not. Keep calling if you need to until you find the one that seems to click.

The bigger the city you choose to work in, the more real estate agents you will have to choose from. You will have everything from your ma and pa local real estate brokerage to your large state brokers. However, this is a system, and we need something that is duplicable. Finding random agents from random agencies is not a system. For this purpose we will work with ReMax real estate franchises. ReMax agents are encouraged to work with investors, as their brokers understand the vital role we play in keeping their business alive.

ReMax agents are paid from a commission, and the more sales they get the higher their take-home percentage. Starting out they may be paying as much as 50% to their broker, but as they increase in sales they may end up keeping 100% of their commission. This is where every agent wants to be. If you are able to buy ten houses a month, do you think they will do whatever necessary to take care of you? I guarantee it. Think about how much volume that would be for them from a single buyer.

To find a ReMax agent you will want to go to ReMax.com. Next, go to the Agents/ Offices tab at the top, click on the Office search tab, and enter city and state. This will pull up the map of all the ReMax offices in your desired area. Click on one of the red balloons and it will pull up that office information. I have to admit that I am a very partial to ReMax, as nearly all the agents I have used have been ReMax agents.

Now it's time to make that call. Try not to be nervous, and in fact you should be feeling good about calling because–believe it or not–real estate agents make their living by selling houses. Real estate is a very dog-eat-dog world, and this real estate agent you are about to call is about to have someone fall into their lap who has a system that is proven to work

When making the call to the office you will get the office secretary. When she answers say...

" Hi, may I speak to the high performing agent in your office?"

You are asking for a high performing agent because you need someone who has an abundance mindset and you need someone who is going to be very well organized. Non-performing agents are not generally either of the above. They are average, just like their paychecks!

Many courses say that it's crucial to find an agent that works with investors. I disagree for a couple reasons. First, if they already deal with a handful of investors, then why would they bring you the deals? Second, you already have a system of how you want things done; you just need someone willing to do it.

Next, the agent will get on the phone and introduce him/herself and ask how they can help you. Say...

"Hi, my name is _____, and I'm interested in buying property in your area. Can you tell me how the market there is doing and specifically where investors are buying and making their money."

Don't say anything about wholesaling, as most agents don't know anything about it, and in fact most of them think it's illegal.

You will want to ask them a handful of questions. This is more so to make them comfortable. The more questions you ask, the more educated you sound and it makes them more comfortable to be working with an educated buyer. Ask them...

- Is it possible to make $20,000 to $30,000 in profits from flipping houses there?

- Is there a specific hot spot for investors right now?

- How is the market compared to six months or a year ago?

- Are there a lot of good deals out there?

- Are there a lot of investors in the area?

That will be enough to get them to talk. Sit back and listen. Pay close attention, because they should be giving you usable information.

Finally, say, "Thank you so much for all the information, but so I can do some further research before diving in can you send me a list of all the cash solds in the area for the past two months, and can you send me what you feel would be your top five deals right now."

After they say "Ok," say, " Thank you, I'll be in touch."

Be sure to leave them your email so they know where to send the information.

What you're doing is testing their work ethic and mindset... that's really all this was for. Do they believe good discount deals are out there to make $30,000 profits? Are they optimistic about plentiful deals? And will they do the work you need in a timely manner?

I generally expect to have all the information that same night or at least by the next morning. If it takes them three days to get it to you, then move on and go through the process again because they won't work out.

Don't make any offers yet, as you still have some homework to do. You don't want to get a property accepted if you don't have the rest of the pipeline set up to complete the deal. As far as the list of "cash solds" that the agent sent you, you'll be using it soon, so for now create a folder in your email and save it there.

Have Your Real Estate Agent Build Another Market for You

This is where this system can start growing really fast. Once you have all the homework done in your market, offers are being made and deals are being done, you can just as easily do all this in another market and have twice the opportunity, and so on. However, I recommend spending plenty of time in one market before moving on just so you have time to get used to it.

When it's time to build another market, this time you can have your A Player real estate agent do it for you. Why would they do that? Because they get a referral fee off of every transaction you do with the new agent. Those referral fees can be up to $500 per transaction. Let's say you end up doing ten deals a month in the second market, and your first real estate agent is now making a residual $5,000 a month. This is why this system works so well, because nearly every angle of it is using leverage as well as creating a win-win for everyone.

I am going to let my top ReMax agent tell how he does this...

First, go to zillow.com and click "find a pro" at the top. Second, click on "real estate agents" and then " buyers agent." Third, enter your desired city and state. This is going to pull up a lot of agents. Finally, go through and find the agents who have the highest number of listings and the highest number of reviews. I recommend a minimum of ten listings and ten reviews. The reviews must be four stars or greater.

This allows you to quickly find the highest performing agents within that specific market. High performing agents will not always be willing to do this system and make all these offers, but there are agents that are willing to work very hard and/or have a staff of people that can do it for them.

Finally, have your current agent contact these new agents and discuss the system you are currently working on. It's up to these two agents to work out how they want to work out the referral fees, but the point is getting them doing this legwork for you.

If for whatever reason your agent doesn't want to build your business with you, then you can use this outline yourself and find high performing agents in any market within minutes.

I'm sure you can see from Shane's outline just how easy this can be. Between Shane's and my outline and scripts you can access any agent in any city within just a few minutes and maybe even have your new real estate agent work on finding your next agent for you. This is faster and more advanced than anything else out there.

Chapter 7: How to Find a Real Estate Attorney

Step 3

The quickest way to find an attorney who can close your wholesale deals is to ask another wholesaler who is doing business in your desired area whom they are using. Remember this system is about efficiency and leverage. By getting information from someone else you are leveraging all the work they have already done to find this attorney. I will show you how to find other wholesalers in the next chapter. Feel free to jump ahead if you want to take this route.

Another way to find a real estate attorney is to go to yp.com, type in "real estate closing attorney" in the first box and your city and state in the second. Once the listings pull up, you can just start calling. Since you will likely not be familiar with any of them there is no need to pick and choose; just pick up the phone and call.

Take a deep breath, pick up the phone, and call. The receptionist will answer. Say, "Hello, my name is _____. Is there an attorney available whom I can speak with?"

Once they answer, say, "Hi, my name is _____. I am looking to do some business in the near future and I am curious if you currently work with any clients who do double closes or assignment of contracts?"

You can be straight to the point because if they work with people that do these they will be familiar with what you are talking about. There is no need to try and educate them.

If they say no, say ok, thanks, and ask if they know anyone that does. Take down the information if provided.

If they say yes, say, "That's great. When I do a double close I like to use the funds from the second transaction to fund the first. Can you do them that way?"

If they say yes, then you have yourself an attorney who can do what you need them to. If they say no, then continue to make phone calls until you get a yes. No exceptions. There are other ways to close deals but they get too messy. Besides, wholesaling is popular enough these days that there should be a couple of attorneys in every major city that will do them this way.

Here is an example of one of my attorneys and why I use them over and over again. I had a closing on a property and my wholesale fee was supposed to be $5,000. When I went to pick up my check it was for around $3,800. Obviously I was kind of like, uhh, where's the rest? Well, because the way they were used to doing things with other wholesalers they did a double closing, and therefore I had fees I had to pay for them having to close the transaction between my buyer and me (more on this in a minute).

After getting discouraged, we sat down and figured out the best way to construct the close to lose as little as possible to closing. The attorney's assistant called me and emailed me a couple different times with different options.

I tell you this to again demonstrate an A Player and how they think. An A Player always has a "how can I" attitude. Always. A B Player or below will just say, "Well, that's not how we do it," or, "It doesn't work that way." They are worlds apart. One of the greatest things about A Players is they pride themselves on being efficient. So with attorneys and their assistants being A Players, along with being very efficient you will have a winning combination.

Below are the two different kinds of closes you will do. For the record I almost always do a double close and you should too. It does cost a little to do them, whereas the assignment of contract doesn't cost you anything, but the double close is cleaner. The attorney does a closing between the seller and yourself then a transaction between you and your buyer. This way you actually do own it even if it's for only a few minutes. Also, with a double close no one sees what you are making. Sometimes when a wholesaler has a hefty profit the buyers on the backside can get a little bitter. They shouldn't but they do.

Assignment of Contract

An assignment of contract is when you get a house under contract (meaning you have a purchase agreement signed between a seller and yourself) and then you sign your rights to that property over to another buyer for a fee. This fee is taken out of the HUD at closing. Assignments of contract cannot be done on bank owned properties or short sales, and they won't even consider accepting an offer on a property if you have this on the purchase agreement. Assignments of contract will generally be done on an owner occupied property or even an investor's home that he is dumping. When doing an assignment of contract you need to have "and/or assigns" behind your name on the purchase agreement.

Double Close

A double close is just as it sounds, two closings back to back. Another word for it is a "simultaneous close." You want your double closings to be "dry," meaning the funds from the second transaction funds the first. If the attorney cannot do them dry, then it means you will have to use transactional funding, which can strip away a lot of your profit. This is why I say to keep calling until you find someone that can do them this way.

So basically this is what a double closing looks like....

1) Assuming all paperwork is signed, your buyer (investor) brings a check to the attorney's office.

The attorney uses your investor's funds for you to close the transaction between the seller (bank or homeowner) and yourself (buyer).

Then the attorney closes the second transaction between you (now the seller) and your buyer (investor).

Out of the proceeds check, the original seller is paid and you are paid your wholesale fee minus whatever your attorney's fees are. In Iowa I have to have abstract run on me since I am selling to make sure there are no liens, and I have to pay the attorney for the closing. The total comes up to around $380.

Like I said, I almost always do a double close. Most of the properties you will offer on will be foreclosures and short sales so you will have to double close those anyway. And you should be trying to get higher and higher wholesale fees. Once you start making $10,000 and more on a wholesale deal, you should be doing double closes so you don't offend your buyers.

For a double close, you can simply use your state bar-approved real estate purchase agreement between you and your buyer and an additional contract between you and the seller. If using a real estate agent, they will have the purchase agreement their brokerage uses. If buying from a homeowner, then you can again use the state approved purchase agreement. Just remember to put "and/or assigns" behind your name. Your attorney will be able to provide you with copies of these purchase agreements or a place to get them.

If you are going to use an assignment of contract, here is an assignment form that assigns the property from you to your buyer.

Assignment of Contract

The undersigned Assignor, having executed a contract dated
_____ between

_____

Contractor, and

_____

Contractee
concerning the property described as:

_____

_____

_____

_____

hereby assigns all rights to said contract to:

_____

("Assignee")

in exchange for compensation in the amount of $_____.

(_____)

Assignee agrees to fulfill all terms, conditions, and contingencies of said Contract and to
perform as required in good faith and within any time periods established by said Contract
this _____ day of _____,

20_____.

_____

Assignor

_____

Witness

_____

Assignee

_____

Witness

Deed Restrictions

A deed restriction is when a bank will not let you sell a property within a certain amount of time of ownership. Deed restrictions can be 30, 60, 90, or even 120 days. This is obviously a hindrance to us, as we need to be able to sell immediately; that is the whole point of this system. Many banks are now going this route as well as short sales, so how do we get around it so we can do our quick close? There are a couple ways.

Short Sale – If you get a counter-offer back from the bank and it looks like it's going to be a deal, you can find your buyer within a day or two and counter back with them on the purchase agreement with you. Then, after closing, you can deed the property over to them. Your attorney can help with all of this. If you get the property accepted without a counter-offer, you can either a) say to your real estate agent that you need to change the business name on the purchase agreement, or b) you can let your buyer know that it's a short sale and has a deed restriction, and ask if they can finance you until the deed restriction passes, and then you can deed it back over to them. If it's a really good deal then they shouldn't have a problem with it.

Foreclosure – If the foreclosure has a deed restriction on it, it can be done the same as above. Another way to do it is to create a new LLC for any new property you are going to wholesale, then have your buyer buy the LLC. When doing this you will want to create the LLC in the name of the address of the property, such as 5555 Quailridge Dr, LLC. I try to never do it this way, as many buyers are leery about buying LLC's. If that is a problem get them in touch with your real estate attorney so they can be assured that the LLC is clean. I don't find that deed restrictions have ever stopped me from getting deals done, and you should be the same way.

If you're going to be successful with this, you have to be willing to get creative and count on the right people to help figure things out. I created this system to be as smooth as possible, but there will still be times when you hit a snag. Just keep your head up and keep moving forward.

Chapter 8: Building Your Buyers List

Step 4

Wholesaling is 100% focused on serving your buyers and bringing them what they need.

Once you grasp that concept, you will skyrocket your income and business. What most wholesalers do is make offers and put out advertising with no rhyme or reason, and then when they get a deal they send it out to everyone on their list. This is not how we are going to do it. Our approach is going to be much more systematic than this.

There are two approaches you can take when sending your deals to your buyers.

1. You send the deals to only your top few buyers first and let them decide, then take it to your larger list should the top buyers not want it.

2. You send your deals to your entire list of buyers and let everyone fight over them.

I started my business going with option one. It was when I was smaller and lazier, but I was still making $50,000 a month doing it this way. When I would get a deal I would send a text to my top buyers and I would usually have it gone in an hour or two. The downside to this approach is your buyers and their buying power change over time. You might have a new guy who is pounding the pavement, raising money, and making his rise as an investor, yet you never send any deals his way because he was never on your original list. Or you may have a more established buyer who decides to retire or not buy as much, limiting your sale potential. Also, if you have your top few buyers, they likely will want to limit your earning potential on each deal.

The second option is what I do and teach now. I would say the reason is that it creates urgency! Word gets around of the deals you're sending out. So when you start sending out these great deals, all the other buyers know that there are many other eyes looking at the deals. Often times, after I send out an email I will have people accept it without even looking at it. Why? One, because I offer great deals, and two, because the buyers know there will be lots of interest. Also, my business is getting large enough to where I can't personalize it anymore. If I limit each deal to a few buyers, then overall I'm limiting my business.

The more buyers you have, the more profit potential you have. If you have one buyer who only buys three-bed ranches for $50,000 to $75,000, then you're limited on wholesaling those kinds of properties, and the likelihood of your finding enough to keep you in business is unlikely. However, if you have dozens or hundreds of buyers that are all looking for something different, then you have yourself an endless number of possibilities.

A Minimum of Five

In my business, I like to have a minimum of five buyers for each different price range and/or type of house. For example, I have my top five who flip starter homes in good neighborhoods and I have my top five who sell on contract. Neighborhoods vary, giving me more flexibility. I have my top five who buy lower income rentals, and I have my top five who buy small multi-plexes.

The reason I have five is it allows for depth, just like a quarterback position on a football team. If that quarterback gets hurt, they will send in the second string. If something should happen to him, then they have a third string. With wholesaling it's similar. Sometimes investors can't buy because all their capital is tied up, maybe they have too many projects going on, maybe they are out of town and can't take a look when you need an answer. There are hundreds of reasons, but point is to have depth to your buyers. Always be paying attention and trying to grow your list. It really hurts when you have to pass on a property because you don't have a buyer for it, and then two weeks later you find a buyer that it would have been perfect for. Be diverse and get to know everyone in the area you are working in. Even if you are doing it remotely, there are still ways to find everyone.

How to Find the Buyers

You should really try to enjoy finding your buyers. The more you find, the more money you will make. There are several ways to find buyers quickly, and some not as quick. I will share these in order of speed, so you can build your buyers' list quickly while adding to it with a couple of the slower but sure routes.

Craiglist.com – This site is a hot spot for real estate and finding your buyers. Go to your desired city and state and click on "real estate for sale" under the housing tab. Next in the search box, type "we buy houses" and hit search. This will give you all kinds of different buyers.

Another search you can do in the same box is type "contract" and click on "by owner" above it, then hit search. This is going to pull up a list of many of the investors who buy and sell houses on contract.

Another way is to click on the "apts/housing" tab under housing. This is going to bring up a huge list of landlords. There may be a few homeowners who you run into, but for the most part it should be almost all investors.

Cash Solds – In Chapter 6 you were told to have your real estate agent send you a list of the last couple of months of cash solds, and this is one of the reasons why. Nearly all the properties on that list were sold to investors that paid cash. Hence the term "cash solds." You can find them by clicking on the listing. The listing will show the address of the property. Next go to the county assessor page of the house you are checking into. Depending on the size of the city you may have a few different county assessor websites you will have to jump between. When you punch the address into the county assessor site, it will pull up the information on that property. What you are looking for is the buyer's home or office address. Write their name or business name down and the mailing address. You will want to go through the whole list of cash solds and do this for each property. Depending on the size of the city and the amount of sales you may need to do only one month of cash solds, then do it again in another month with a newer list of cash solds.

Google – Type in "house buyers" or "we buy houses," plus your city and state.

If you are wholesaling in the area you live, here are a few options.

- Call off for rents signs.

- Call rent ads in the daily or Sunday paper.

- Go to the local REI (real estate investment group).

- Go to the real estate auctions.

The first two steps should get you all the buyers you need to get going. Go through the cash solds once a month. Each time should get easier as you will be constantly adding to your list and you will recognize many of the names when going through the assessor page. Once you have them as a buyer you don't need to send them any more letters. Go through Craigslist once a week at first to see if you can pick up any more names and numbers.

Teaming With Other Wholesalers

I remember when I first got started in this business I always thought of the other investors as my competition. Now I realize it's just the opposite. Finding other wholesalers will give you opportunities for even more deals. You should get to know every wholesaler in the area! There may be times, especially in the beginning, when you are short on buyers. This is an excellent time to team up with other wholesalers. Teaming up with wholesalers in multiple areas is a way to increase your income like crazy. Assuming you are networking with experienced wholesalers, you can find deals in any market throughout the country and get the deals done without even having any buyers. I would say it's equally important to have a network of wholesalers as it is to have your own buyers.

Other wholesalers will also be able to hook you up with the best attorneys for double closes. Sometimes they will even be willing to share their buyers. Network, network, network. Everyone out there has something that can benefit you. It may not show itself for a long time, but the more people you know the better off you'll be.

Create a Database

As your database of buyers continues to grow, you'll need an appropriate way to keep things organized and efficient. In the beginning you can get yourself a large three-ring binder and a three-hole punch from an office store, and make copies of the following lead sheet. This may even be sufficient for as long as you stay in business, depending on how large you decide to get. I highly recommend always keeping a tangible file. It will be a terrible day when you go to your computer and everything somehow gets deleted. Always keep a written backup. If you prefer, periodically print out hardcopies of your spreadsheets and keep them in folder.

Once you are doing really high volume, whether it's in just your city or many cities, you will benefit from an online newsletter system. This way you can import all your buyers' emails, and when you get a property accepted you can send out the wholesale package and the nicely crafted newsletter will be sent out to all your buyers. One great ad source to use it Postlets.com. With this website you can "post" your deal and submit it to your buyers, but you can also publish it on all the real estate websites such as zillow.com and trulia.com. This allows anyone on these websites to see your deals, which can get you a deal closed or at least bring you more buyers.

There are many newsletter sources... here are a few to check out.

- Campaigner.com

- mailchimp.com

- icontact.com

- campaignmonitor.com

- activecampaign.com

- constantcontact.com

- zoho.com

Below is your buyers lead sheet. In case you meet another buyer or a buyer makes a return call, you should always have a couple with you.

If you are at all new to this, don't be nervous when calling these buyers. They are people just like you and me. I remember being really nervous when calling them the first few times. I'm sure it was the insecurity of not knowing exactly what I was doing. The most important thing to know is that they *want* you to call! It's guaranteed that other wholesalers have already called them, so they are used to it, and it won't be anything new to them.

With this lead sheet below you are simply finding out what kinds of deals they like so you know what to bring to them when you get a deal.

Also, don't try to pretend to be something you're not. If you're new to this it's ok to admit that... every one of them started at a beginning point too.

Investor Lead Sheet

Name:

Business Name:

Email:

Phone#:

What areas do you buy in?

Do you flip, hold or sell on contract?

What types of properties do you like?

What's your price range?

How much profit do you need from each deal?

Are repairs ok? How much?

How quickly can you close?

How many deals can you handle a month?

What would you like in the packets I send you?

Are you ok putting up the earnest money?

Notes:

Letter to Investors

Your name or business name

Your address

City, St 55555

Dear Real Estate Investor,

My name is (your name) and I am real estate wholesaler. I noticed you recently bought property in the (city) area. That area is also an area that I am always scouting for properties. I have a unique system for finding really good, undervalued real estate deals. Because my system works so well to find these great deals I often have numerous properties each month that I need to unload to buyers like yourself. I pride myself on putting together excellent deals as I want you to make great profits. In my experience this makes for a great relationship. Please contact me asap so we can discuss your business and how I can be of service . My number is 555-5555.

Thanks, and I look forward to speaking with you soon.

Respectfully,

(your name)

Chapter 9: Finding the Deals

Step 5

First off, I want to give a lot of credit to my rock star real estate agent for helping come up with this system. My unique ability is creating visions and finding other people to create the systems to execute those visions. I like to dream stuff up and see if it can be put it into action, whereas Shane, my agent, is excellent at systems, analyzing, and taking something from creation to completion. This entire system was taken from vision to reality over a lunch with my real estate agent.

This offering system is based solely on a numbers game: the more offers you write, the more you will get. I base my offers on a 25:1 system as I was originally taught. Now, historically I have achieved a much better percentage than this, but many times I was buying too high. If you are offering low enough so that it's both a good deal for your buyer and a nice spread for you, then you are on target.

I also like the 25:1 system because it allows for easier calculation. For example, if you want to make $10,000 a month and average $5,000 per deal, then it would make sense that you would need to make fifty offers. If you want to make $50,000 a month, then it would make sense that you would need to write 250 offers. If you are doing that much volume, you'll need to be doing business in at least a couple of markets.

But you see the point–it's all a numbers game. Decide on what you want or need to make and adjust accordingly. I advise keeping the goals somewhat modest for the short term so you can get the kinks worked out in your market, but once you get the hang of it, take it full speed. There's no reason you couldn't be handling three or four markets at once.

The Three Ways to Find Deals

You are going to be using three different techniques to finding your deals. There are dozens of ways to find deals and they all work, but to have a finely tuned system there has to be simplicity to it and ease of use. Therefore this system has been narrowed down to the following...

1) MLS (multiple listing system)

2) Bandit signs

3) Craigslist

Power of the MLS

Many wholesalers don't utilize the MLS the way they should. Instead they spend all kinds of money advertising in hopes that people will come to them with a house. Then they hope that they can buy it low enough to make a deal work. Now I'm not dogging them, because that method can work, but it costs a lot more, takes a lot longer, and generally creates fewer deals.

It's proven that up to 80% of the deals will be on market deals, meaning on the MLS. So if up to 80% of your deals are going to be on the MLS, wouldn't it make sense to use it to it's absolute fullest? Here's a comparison example of leverage and cost.

Wholesaler A

Spends $1,500 on 5,000 postcards and gets one deal.

Spends $1,500 on commercials and gets one deal.

Spends $1,500 on other ads and gets one deal.

Wholesaler B

Has three markets developed and has 200 offers a month being made between them, and gets eight deals. He spends nothing and his real estate agent made all the offers for him.

Which wholesaler would you want to be? I have been the wholesaler who has paid for signs, TV commercials, print ads, etc., and the amount of deals I get off the MLS compared to all those off-market ways is not even comparable. As a wholesaler going the traditional route of paying for advertising, you can easily spend thousands or tens of thousands of dollars for the same amount of deals you will get off the MLS. I have seen many markets where almost all of the wholesalers were not using the MLS! And most of the other investors were only writing a handful of offers a month. What this leaves is a huge opportunity for deals and profit.

In my markets I have an offer on every single foreclosure, short sale, estate sale, and distressed property on the market. I am going to show you how to set up the same system.

The MLS is primarily what this system is based on. The other two avenues are additional ways to acquire properties and they are excellent ways to find deals, but you definitely need to spend the time getting your agent set up on making these offers on the MLS.

Bandit Signs

Wholesalers are notorious for using bandit signs and there is a good reason... it gets the phone ringing! The deals you get from the off-market deals such as bandit signs can be some of your best deals. The MLS is for consistent deals, but the bandit signs and Craigslist are for your home-run deals.

Bandit signs are the rectangular yard signs you see along the road that say "We Buy Houses," or something to that degree. It's known in this industry that the 18 x 24 yellow sign with black ink is the most effective tool for pulling in leads. Most say to handwrite on both sides of each sign with a fat black sharpie. I did this for a couple of hundred signs and almost passed out from the marker fumes. It didn't take me long before I was searching for a way to make it more efficient. So I called an online sign production shop and asked them if I could send one of my signs and have them make a copy of the sign and hold it on file so they could print them off and make them look handwritten. I didn't even have to do that. Instead I wrote out "We Buy Houses" with a chisel tip sharpie on an 8x11 sheet of paper horizontally and scanned that over to them. They had a perfect proof back to me that same day. Going this route is going to save you so much time.

The best sign shop I have found to this point is www.dirtcheapsigns.com. Go to the website and call them and let them know that you want to go the route listed above.

Why use hand-lettered signs and not signs with professional lettering? It's been time tested that hand lettering pulls in more leads. The experts believe it has to do with traditional corporate marketing being shoved down everyone's throat. Hand lettering looks more local, so the caller perceives that it's more likely they'll speak with a live person in the area.

I pay just under $600 for 200 double-sided signs and the 15" stakes. To start out, try buying 100 signs once every two weeks and hang fifty per week. This may be too much money for you starting out, and that is fine. Use the MLS, do a couple of deals, and then use some of the profit money to start growing your business.

I recommend getting a local Google voicemail number for your bandit signs. This is to avoid the wrath of the dreaded city enforcement. I don't know of a single area in the country that likes these signs. In some cities they'll threaten with a fine, and other cities will just take them down. I have put out thousands and thousands of signs and have never had a fine. With the Google voicemail number it's untraceable and it doesn't plug up your cell phone voicemail system. You can go to https://www.google.com/voice to sign up for your new voicemail system.

I started out putting out all the signs myself. It generally took about two hours per twenty-five signs. Although this doesn't seem like much time it's still not being productive. After a while I turned them over to someone I could trust. I pay one dollar per sign to my people who hang signs, and then I pay an additional $250 for any deal I get off the sign. That way I can keep my expenses low on the front end and reward them on the back end.

Depending on the size of the city you're working in, you can decide how many to put out per week. I now average about one hundred per week per city. I started with only about twenty-five and found I wasn't getting the calls I wanted.

Put the signs anywhere people are slowing down or coming to a stop where they will have to wait for a while. Exit ramps, busy street corners, and close to schools are all good spots for the signs.

If you're working a distant city, you can find someone on Craigslist to place them for you. Post an ad and be sure to let them know that you will be paying after the signs are hung. For proof you can have them snap a pic of each location they hang them. Don't ever get to the point where you just figure your sign guys are being honest and you quit checking on them, because they will start to slack. Keep a system in place so they know they are being held accountable. Another option is to have them write down the locations of all the signs and have them email that list to you, then forward it to your real estate agent and ask them to take a drive by a few of the locations to see if they're there.

Hang or have your signs hung on Friday nights. This way your signs will be up all through the weekend without the city enforcement taking them down. You may get some spots where they last for days even weeks, but count on most of them being down within a few days after hanging. It seems like a hassle, but when you have someone else doing it all for you it starts to get a lot easier, and it's well worth it if you can snag even one deal every time you put them out. With only a deal a week you're talking about making $260,000 a year.

Remember that 1 deal = $5,000 x 52 weeks = $260,000.

Would you like to make that kind of income just from having someone hang signs for you once a week?

Craigslist

Craigslist.com has been, and probably always will be, an excellent avenue to find deals. The number of views and posts to Craigslist each day is staggering. The biggest issue that users have is they don't know how to weed through the junk. I remember one of my mentors telling me about Craigslist when I first started but he didn't teach me how to filter out the junk, so each time I went there I would sort through hundreds of listings, none of which seemed like a good deal, and soon enough I got burned out and didn't use it again for years.

Now I know how to use it and how to maximize my time there. Craigslist results will be similar to bandit signs–you can expect to get maybe a deal a week if you are keeping up with it and follow my directions. But again, that could be another $5,000 per week just from looking through ads. So just by using Craigslist and bandit signs you could be looking at over $500,000 per year. That is not exaggerating, that is very realistic!

First, go to www.craigslist.com and click on your desired state and city. Next click on the "real estate for sale" tab. Next type in motivated seller + (your city) in the search box, and click the "by owner" tab above it. That one search is going to reduce all the high price retail listings as well as on-market listings. Most will still be too high, but start making phone calls to find out the sellers' motivations. By adding your city to it you will also eliminate all the garbage that isn't actually in your target area. You can continue through with as many other key word searches as you like. Here are a few examples that will pull up the majority of motivated sellers...

- Motivated seller

- Must sell

- Price reduced

- Estate

- Make offer

It will only take you a half-hour to go through all of these searches. Well worth the effort once a day to make an extra $5,000 a week.

Okay, so there you have it–these are the three different ways that you will go about finding deals. I am going to go deeper into the offering system with the MLS, but I wanted to show you how the deals will come in. With this system the only thing you're spending money on is the bandit signs, and you can wait to do that until after you make a profit from the others.

Think about how leveraged this is. You have a real estate agent who is making all the offers for you. You have someone else who should be hanging all your signs for you, and you only need to look at listings of motivated sellers once a day for twenty minutes and call the ones that look like possible deals.

I really am trying to make this as simple as possible. In fact, I have other wholesalers asking me all the time how I do so many deals and make such high profits. I do exactly this! I don't do any other form of advertising. I like to keep my costs to a minimum and my leverage to a maximum.

Negotiating With Homeowners

Negotiating a price on real estate can be one of the most intimidating things for a new wholesaler. It's understandably so. I remember when I was getting started, and I would get calls from my advertising and have to go out to the owner's house, come up with estimates, and make an offer. All but the latter part was easy. The most important point you can understand is *you don't have to get every deal*, and you won't! If you get one in twenty-five offers you make, you are on target. My ratio with homeowners vs. my ratio with on-market properties does not change.

If you go into the deal with the understanding that you will likely not get the deal, then you don't try so hard to get it. After I make my offer on a house I no longer think about it. It is out of my mind. When you try to hard to get the deal all you do is offer too high, resulting in not being able to get the deal *sold*.

A golden rule in negotiating says that the person who gives the number first, loses. I do try to practice by that rule, but I don't let a negotiation get uncomfortable if the homeowner won't offer up a number.

It's also important to understand the psychology of negotiation and the mindset of the seller. What you're really trying to figure out is the seller's motivation. If they are really motivated you will hear stuff like...

- I just want to move on...

- I inherited it and need to get rid of it...

- My husband left me and I can't afford it...

- We moved my mother to a nursing home and need to sell the house to pay for it...

- We got a job offer and need to move quickly...

I have encountered all these examples and they do prove to be highly motivated sellers. You will get the other calls where someone will say,

- I just want to see what your offer would be...

- We are just checking our options...

- We have an agent coming out to give us her opinion...

These are time wasters! They never result in deals. When I qualify my leads and hear these comments I give them a low offer and send them on their way. I want my time spent on leads that have the best chances of turning into deals. When qualifying a lead, I start with the least invasive questions first and merge into the tougher questions once I have their attention and a rapport is established.

This lead sheet will get you all the information you need on the property. At the bottom of the page I mention about asking for seller financing. If your buyers don't have to get any financing or use their cash to purchase the house this can be a great way to get a wholesale done without having to get it at a very low price.

You can use the following questions for qualifying a lead:

Qualifying a Lead

What is your name?

What is the best number to call you back at?

What is the address?

Can you tell me a little bit about it?

Beds:
Baths:
Sq. Ftg:
Garage:
What is the condition of the property?

Can I ask why you are selling?

Is there still a mortgage on the house?

Are the payments and taxes current? If no, how far behind?

What price do you need to let the house go?

If I can't pay that amount, is the price negotiable? (Everything is negotiable.)

If your price is far below theirs and there is no chance of getting them down, ask if they will carry the financing if you meet their price. This is only if they can't come down.

Setting Up Your Offering System

Your offering system is going to be strongest when you have an A Player real estate agent who takes control of it and makes it part of their daily regimen. As I said before, this is a numbers game, and the more offers you make the more deals you will get. Your real estate agent doesn't have to know that you are going to be wholesaling these. All they need to know is that if the deal is good enough, you can do as many deals a month as they can find for you.

Since wholesaling revolves around your buyers, you will always be limited to how many deals your buyers can handle and how diverse their real estate needs are. For example, if you only have two buyers and they both like good quality houses in good neighborhoods in the $50,000 range, then you can't have your real estate agent making offers on low-income rental properties or high-end flips. So like I said in the buyers' section, the larger database of buyers you have the larger variety of houses you can have your agent offer on. In my area I know enough investor buyers to where there is almost no limit on what they will buy. Therefore, I have my real estate agent putting out offers on every distressed property on the market. But don't wait to get going. Don't wait until you have a large database. Find a handful of buyers and get your agent searching for deals for them right away. As you add more buyers you can have your agent expand the search.

Getting Your Agent Ready to Launch

In the previous paragraphs I mentioned that your real estate agent doesn't have to know you are wholesaling. That is true, but I would try to ease them into knowing as soon as possible so everyone is on the same page. Just ask them to keep it between you guys so everyone isn't trying to do it. Trying to get your real estate agent to make offers for you should not be too tough if you have the right agent. If they submit a couple of offers on your behalf, most would be ok with it, but when you are talking dozens or hundreds of offers a month they will want to feel protected, as it's not common practice to make all these offers on their clients' behalf. In fact my real estate agent wanted me to get a "power of attorney" for him and his agency.

The limited power of attorney letter basically protects your real estate agent should something happen from them making all the offers. It says that you gave them permission to do this. Here is a sample power of attorney letter that my real estate attorney had drawn up... this is not legal advise, please consult your own attorney.

Power of Attorney Letter

The undersigned, (your name), (your business name if applicable), of (city and state), do hereby make, constitute and appoint my real estate agent(s) (real estate agent's name) of (real estate agent's brokerage) the undersigned's true and lawful Attorney-in-Fact, with full right, power and authority to act for the undersigned and in the undersigned's name, place and stead as to the following actions:

(Real estate agent's name) have the authority to sign and execute and sign on my behalf Purchase Agreement and corresponding documents related to the acquisition of property for (your name or business name).

This authority is limited to the initial contractual documents that shall bind me to purchase of property. The authority does not extend to the sale of any of my properties.

This Power of Attorney is not affected by subsequent disability or incapacity of the principal. It's the principal's intent that the authority given to the Attorney in fact may be exercised even if the Principal becomes disabled or incapacitated.

Giving and Granting unto said Attorney-In-Fact the full power and authority to do and perform each and every act, deed, matter and thing whatsoever required and necessary to be done in and about the foregoing, as fully as the undersigned might or could do if personally present and acting.

The undersigned further directs that this Power of Attorney shall take effect immediately and shall be irrevocable unless and until such time as there is filed of record a duly acknowledged revocation of this instrument in the same office in which the instrument containing this power is recorded.

The Power granted under this Power of Attorney is granted to (real estate agent's) severally and each can act individually to sign on my behalf without the need for the other Power of Attorney's consent.

The undersigned does hereby authorize said Attorney-in-Fact to relinquish all rights of dower, homestead and distributive share and to any real estate described herein in which the undersigned Words and phrases herein, including acknowledgment hereof, shall be construed as in the singular of plural number, and as masculine or feminine gender, according to the context.

Dated: _____

_____

Grantor, (your name), (member/manager business name)
State of (your state)
County of (your county)

This instrument was acknowledged before me on (date), by (your name, member/manager of business name)

_____

Notary Public in and for the State of (your state)

Proof of Funds Letter (POF)

For a new wholesaler, a proof of funds letter can be about the toughest part. First off, a proof of funds letter does not say that you are guaranteed or approved for funds; that would be a pre-approval letter. People get pre-approval letters from the bank when they are approved for financing. A proof of funds letter can be from any financial institution or person that has the ability to fund your transaction. Your real estate agent will most likely want to send one in for each offer they make on your behalf. This is why I try to have them made as vague as possible and dated out as far as possible.

If possible, try to bypass this by asking your agent to submit offers, and say that you will get them a POF letter for each property that gets countered or accepted. It really shouldn't be a problem. When I sell houses I get offers all the time without the pre-approval letter and then they send that a couple of days later. So this is no different. If your agent is willing to work it this way then you are good to go. The one site I know of that produces free POF letters is www.besttransactionalfunding.com. They are a transactional funding company, which is basically an extended double closing that we discussed earlier. However, their funds are real and can be backed up and that is all a POF letter is.

If you have a real estate agent who is not willing to submit without a POF letter, then you need someone who can get one for you. If you know anyone who has enough money in the bank, 401k's, IRAs, private lenders, etc.–anyone who has enough money can have one made for you from their institution if they tell their financial institution that they plan to loan to you on secured real estate.

Another route is to ask any of the investors you call when building your buyers list if they can provide a POF letter so you can get deals accepted and bring deals to them. Assure them that if they help you out by doing this favor that you will repay the favor by giving them first dibs on your deal (and stick to your promise).

Here is an example of a generic POF letter.

(Letterhead)

October 15, 2013

To Whom It May Concern,

Mark Lane and/or Lane Investments, LLC have funds available up to $100,000 with (Lender/ Financial Institution)

Thank You,

(Their signature)

(Their printed name)

(Their position)

Inspection Period

Having your inspection period in place is your safety net for wholesaling. It's your out should you not be able to get rid of it. If you are getting a great deal you should never have to use your full inspection period. The standard inspection period for an on-market deal is going to be ten days. Some people say to try and extend that out another four to five days, but I have never seen the point in that. Like I said, if it's a good enough deal, then you should have it sold right away.

Also, I have never exercised my inspection period as a reason for not getting a deal. If for whatever reason I don't have a good enough deal for my buyers, then I will go back to the seller and ask for a "credit due to cost of required repairs." When I ask for that credit, that will almost always kill the deal itself, which is ok because it wasn't a good enough deal to begin with. The credit I ask for may be as high as $10,000. However, before I ask for any credit I will first ask any buyers who have interest what they would be willing to pay for it. This gives me a number to ask for less my wholesale fee. Don't be afraid to do this; it's much better than going to the end of your inspection period and then dumping it without cause.

Handwritten Offers

If your real estate agent still writes all their offers by hand, you may consider shopping around for a new agent. If you're going to use an agent who submits handwritten offers then you need to know how to help them be more efficient. First, any contract they write for you is going to be 99% the same as the one before it. Really, the only thing that is going to change in each offer is the address, the price, and the date. They should be able to create a template that they can save to their computer in your file and when they need to make an offer they just input the difference in price and the new address and hit print.

To set this up they just need to send you a blank purchase agreement. You go through and sign and initial where applicable and send back. If they are technology challenged like myself, you can have a stamp of your signature and initial made at Office Depot for a few bucks, get the order number, and give it to the real estate agent and have them pick it up at their nearest location. They can use this stamp to take care of any addendums or such at any time.

Going Digital

Yes, the real estate industry has been forever changed by technology, and in fact that is exactly why we are able to implement this system and do everything virtually. It's crazy what's now available to us. If you aren't getting rich these days with how easy things are, then you just don't know how or you aren't trying.

Most real estate agents and brokers are now writing their offers digitally through e-signature websites. Docusign and Dotloop are two of the most widely used. They are basically paperless forms of the purchase agreement contract that the real estate brokers use or used to use. It does cut down on a ton of paperwork and ink and time by not having to print out each offer. These e-signature websites are all the same concept–once your agent sends it to you, hit start or next field and it automatically takes you through each field where you need to input information. Although they are a breakthrough for the industry and a time saver they can still be a major pain. Would you want to have to go through twenty offers every night and submit all the information they ask for? I hope not. Why would you when your agent can and will do it for you?

My real estate agents and I we set up a Gmail.com account that we all had access to and they would send the Docusign or Dotloop contract to that specific email, and then they would go back in there themselves and fill out all the information that was intended for me. They can do this because of the power of attorney.

This is the kind of leverage I have been talking about. I hope you are starting to see the power in this system. Through leveraging each aspect of this system you're always able to continually *build* your business rather than working in your business.

Chapter 10: Going Live

Everything up to this point has been building your team, understanding the basics, finding deals, and prepping your real estate agent. Now it's time to go live, so we're going to go through the spreadsheets, which is what this system is all about. My agent and I created these spreadsheets for a few reasons.

1. For the sake of record keeping. Before spreadsheets, I would get offers accepted or countered and my agent would send me emails letting me know, and I wouldn't have any clue what the offer was or when it was made. So by using the spreadsheets I can now open them up and see exactly what we offered on, the address, and the accepted price.

2. Analyze results. At least equally important, we need to know what our offers are telling us. If you are making fifty offers and not getting anything accepted, then you are offering too low or your market is too strong. If you are getting too many accepted or maybe not getting as large wholesale fees as you would like, then you are likely offering too much. By analyzing your offers every week you are able to see what's going on in your market and where the sweet spot is.

3. Manageability. If you're working a few or more markets at a time, it's really nice to be able to pull up the spreadsheets and see how many offers your real estate agent is making. If you're in a large city and your agent is only making five offers a week, then you know that they are not working hard enough and it's time to find a new one. Also, it's nice while you're taking time off or traveling to pull up your spreadsheets and see that offers are still being made on your behalf.

Let's now take a look at the spreadsheets.

Spreadsheet A

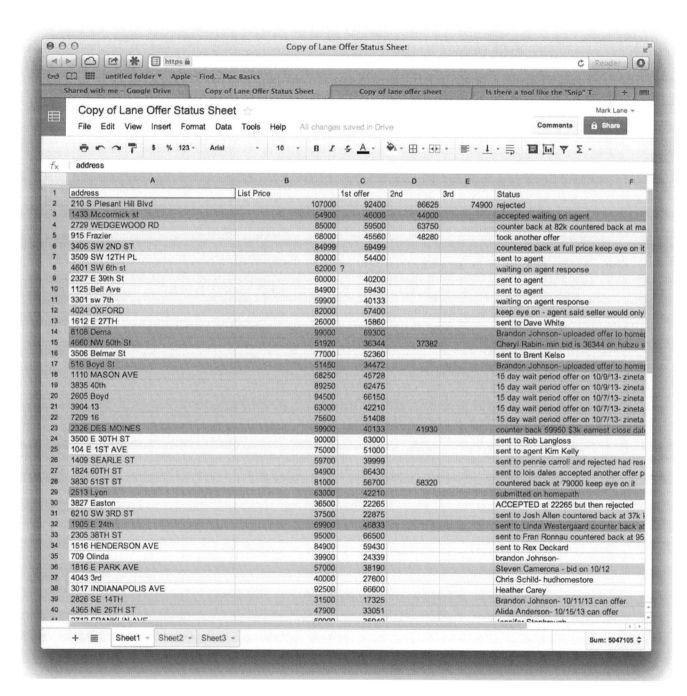

Spreadsheet B

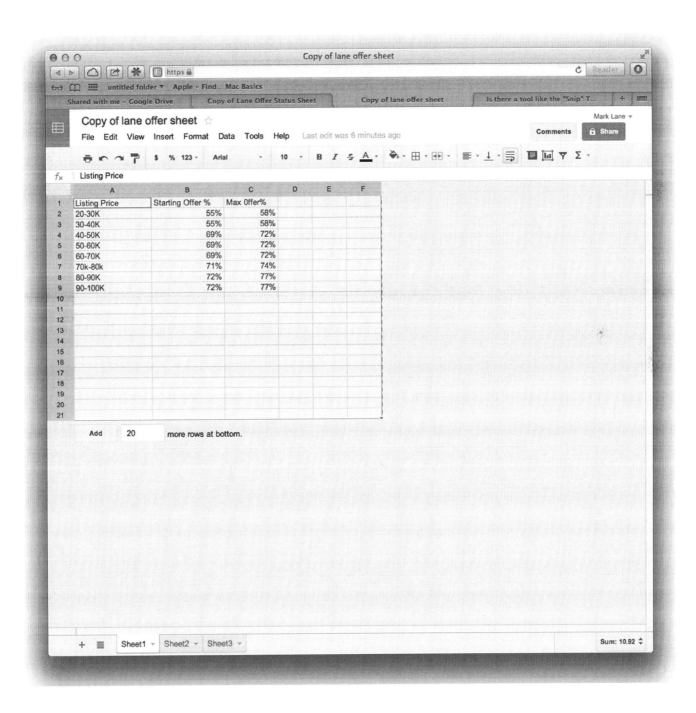

Listing Price	Starting Offer %	Max Offer%
20-30K	55%	58%
30-40K	55%	58%
40-50K	69%	72%
50-60K	69%	72%
60-70K	69%	72%
70k-80k	71%	74%
80-90K	72%	77%
90-100K	72%	77%

How to Set Up the Spreadsheets

Google Drive is nearly the same as Microsoft Excel, so if you have used Excel before then you won't have any problem. If you have never used a computer before, then ask a fourth grader for help. You will need to set up the Google account for you and your agent to share. You should plan to have a few markets going on so you may want to use an email that is somewhat duplicable for ease of use, such as <u>Marksdsmdeals [at] google.com</u>. This way each time you build another market you can just change the abbreviation for the city and leave everything else the same. Once you are doing business in more than one market you can create a new account but have it hosted by your original Gmail account; this way you can log into one email and access your spreadsheets from several cities.

When building your offer sheet you will need to have columns for:

– Address

– List price

– 1st offer

– 2nd offer

– 3rd offer

– Status

My agent color coded these accordingly:

Green = accepted

Yellow= active

Blue = waiting period

Red = closing

You can build yours just like mine. I have yet to run into a problem with this spreadsheet–it's built for simplicity. One thing I am having added is a column for:

F = foreclosure, s = shortsale, e = estate, o = other. This way I will be able to see where most of my deals are coming from.

When building your offer percentage sheet, you will need columns for:

– Listing price

– Starting offer %

– Max offer %

Again, this is built for simplicity, so don't overcomplicate it. Ok, so let's get into these spreadsheets and see exactly what they tell us and how to use them in any market.

Spreadsheet A

At first glance you might say that this spreadsheet is giving us all the details of our offers such as address, list price, offer price, and status, and that is true. But it's also telling us what the market is doing and what the investors are doing.

According to my spreadsheet, it's telling me that the investors on average are buying at 77% of list price or higher. I know this because from spreadsheet B my highest offer percentage is 77%, and according to spreadsheet A, I am only getting about a 25:1 ratio. As I said earlier, you will want to aim for a 25:1 ratio or close to it. According to this spreadsheet I am performing just under that. Therefore that tells me that I need to increase my percentage by a couple of points.

This spreadsheet is also telling me that the market is pretty strong because of my ratio of offers made to offers accepted, as well as my percentages of list price on those offers. If, for example, I am wholesaling in Scottsdale, Arizona, the hottest market in the country, my percentages might have to get adjusted to 80-90% and I may end up getting only 35:1 on my offers. Then the stats tell me that I need to bump up my percentages even a little higher to get closer to the 25:1. If I am in a slower market using the same percentages as the Des Moines (DSM) market, I may end up getting a 10:1 ratio of offers made to deals accepted, and that would tell me that I need to decrease my percentages so my offers are lower and therefore getting less deals accepted.

You might ask, why would I want to get fewer deals accepted? The answer is it that depends on if the deal is good enough for an investor and if there is a good enough wholesale fee to be made. My ratio is consistent at 25:1, and I keep it that way because when I get those deals accepted they are generally so good that I make a larger wholesale fee and the deal is sold to another investor within an hour.

I know some wholesalers who create really skimpy deals, and then they have to market them for a week or two to dozens or hundreds of buyers before they get them sold. I don't want you to work that hard. The goal is to make you as much money with as little work as possible.

Spreadsheet B

This spreadsheet is created to give your real estate agents a guide to what price to make your offers. The reason the percentages change from lower to higher is due to the quality of houses and neighborhoods. I'm going to use the DSM market, for example:

The bottom of my market is $30,000 and below. If I'm making offers of 70% of $30,000, that only brings my accepted offer price to $21,000. Assuming there are plenty of repairs to do there is no value, especially after you try to tack an additional wholesale fee to it. However, if I'm making offers of 55%, then I'm looking at getting it accepted at $16,500, and chances are I could mark it up to at least $18,500 and probably $21,000 and sell it off right away.

Keep in mind that these are almost always going to be distressed properties or at least motivated sellers so generally they will all ready be on the market somewhat under market value.

As we go up in price range, we're also going up in the percentage of our offer price. If we're getting a property that is listed at $100,000 for $72,000-$77,000, chances are we're getting a great deal, because it's likely that the property is already listed under market value, then we sneak in and get it another 23%-28% off.

How To Know Your Percentages

Ok, so now some of the preliminary work you already did is going to come into play. In Chapter 6 you learned how to find a real estate agent and were told to have them send you a list of cash-solds in the last month or two. By understanding the cash-solds, you will be able to understand at what price point investors are buying these properties.

Let's take a look at an example.

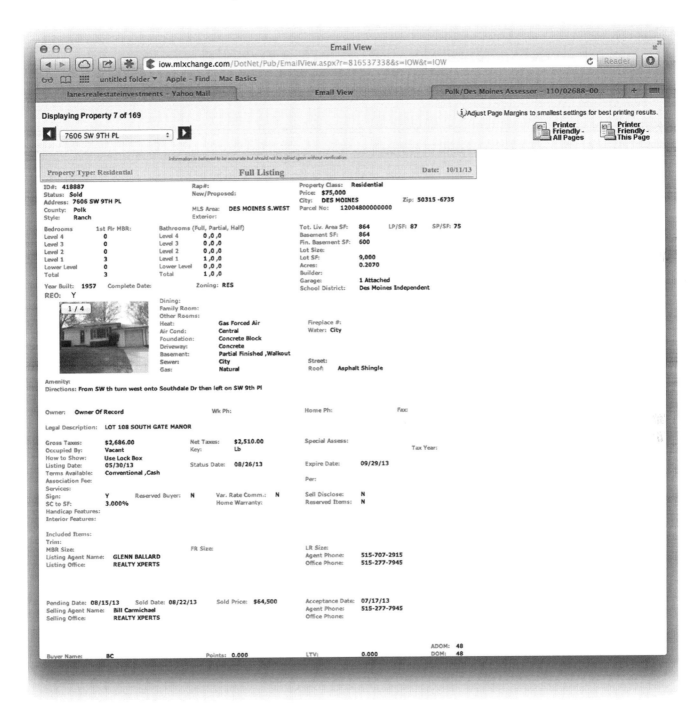

If you look at the top right you will see the list price of $75,000. At the bottom middle will be the sold price of $64,500.

The formula we will use to understand our cash sold's value is:

Sale Price / List Price = Percentage of List Price

Assuming you have your list of cash sold's, go ahead and run through some using that formula. Note: The MLS of every market is different, so your list of cash sold's may look nothing like this; however, it will have all the same information.

To get a really good feel for where your market percentage is, you should go through at least ten in each price range. I prefer to do as many as fifty, to get a really good feel. Write them down, such as...

77%

72%

66%

82%

102%

73%

105%

62%

74%

76%

This strategy goes all the way back to third grade math. Take out all the highs and lows, then take an average of the remaining core numbers. So out of these we would get rid of (in order) 66, 102, 105, and 62. This gives us six numbers to get and average.

77 + 72 + 82 + 73 + 74 + 76 = 454

454 / 6 = 75.66%

This leads us to our average cash sold of 75.66% of list price.

When you get into the lower priced homes, you may notice that the percentage does not go down, and in fact it may go up, but that doesn't mean your offer price should go up with it. Remember the example earlier: Whether it's $10,000 or $100,000, the price to fix it up is going to be relatively the same, which means the cheaper houses have to be bought at a lower percentage in order to create enough of a spread and provide you a wholesale fee.

So now you have your cash-sold percentage of 75.66%. Now you need to determine what your actual offer percent needs to be. If on average your investor is buying at 75.66%, then you can't make your offers at that same percentage, as there is no room for your fee. Instead you need to drop that percentage down maybe five or ten percent. So now you have your starting offer percentage of 68%-70% of the list price.

In order to provide a small amount of flexibility, you can include a range such as spreadsheet B. This will give your real estate agent a percentage to start at, but a maximum they can't go over, at least not without your permission.

My agents know to contact me whenever there is a counter offer within a close proximity of the range, and at that point I can decide to proceed or not.

Properties

Before your real estate agent starts making offers for you, it's important to understand what you will be making offers on, why those properties, and how frequently will you be making them.

You have to have keyword searches for your real estate agent to search so they can be utilizing their time and your system optimally. Have them search the following:

Foreclosures – Bank-owned properties will always be available and they will always be able to be bought at somewhat of a discount. The colder a market is, the more foreclosures will be in surplus. The hotter a market is, the fewer there will be and the more they will be in demand. Our country is in a massive financial crisis, which will lead to higher taxes, rising prices of healthcare, inflation, increased prices of goods, etc. And as this all happens it's going to bankrupt a lot of people, leading them into foreclosure. It's unfortunately a daily occurrence. Financial intelligence is missing in modern society, and people like you will have the tools to pick up these properties for a fraction of what they are worth.

Short Sales – A short sale is where the bank is willing to take less on the property than what the current owner owes. They do this to try and avoid the property going into foreclosure. It costs the mortgage holders a lot of money when properties go into foreclosure, so they are doing everything they can to prevent it. After the burst of the last housing bubble, short sales became very popular as everyone was searching for a way to avoid foreclosure and because there were so many owners upside down with their houses. Many of my best deals have been short sales. I especially like them when the bank accepts my low offer without even being countered. One blessing of short sales is if you have your offer in first, the bank will entertain your offer first and all other offers will have to be held as back-up. This is opposed to offering on foreclosed properties, where many investors bid on the same property at the same time, creating lots of competition, which drives the price even higher.

Estate Sales – I love estate sales. My lowest accepted offers historically have been estate sales. I often make these between 50%-60% of list price because my averages of getting them low have been so good. With an estate sale, someone has inherited the property after the owner has passed away. The new owners very often want nothing to do with the property. They have their own life, often times out of state, and they don't want to go through the hassle of owning another property, fixing it up, paying taxes, holding utilities, etc. Also, to the average person, getting a check of even $20,000 or more can seem like winning the lottery, so when they get an all-cash offer and they see a nice profit they get excited and let the property go. Most of them don't even care about holding out for a much higher offer.

Make Offer – Occasionally there will be listings that say, "make offer." These are generally homeowners who are desperate to sell for one reason or another. Could be a medical issue and they need cash immediately, could be a job relocation, maybe an older couple moving south and they know there is a lot of work to be done on the house. There could be dozens of reasons why an owner would list their house this way. The important thing is that you meet their request and make an offer.

Price Reduced – In a minute you will see how we keep track of our offers, but for now let's understand a price reduced listing. Logically a person would only reduce their price if they are motivated. If they aren't motivated at all, they would just keep at the same price until they get an offer or the contract expires. Once your real estate agent makes the first offers, they will pin that listing so it automatically updates anytime there is a status change with it. If the same property drops in price a two or three times, then you know that the seller is getting really motivated to move that property.

By concentrating on these kinds of properties you will increase your chances of getting the low offers accepted. Also, you are dealing with mostly banks or highly motivated sellers who don't care about the property. Banks only look at the numbers there is no emotional attachment there. The same goes for the rest of them most of the time.

Automatic Searches

If you have ever worked with a real estate agent before you will know that it's common practice for them to set you up on an automatic search that shuttles any matching criteria directly to your email. When building this system, my agent and I figured it was best to have my agent set them up so they would go to him instead. This way I'm not bogged down with hundreds of offers each day. My real estate agent has the criteria set up to go to him, and then when he gets the emails he sends them over to one of his associates who makes the offers and enters status into the spreadsheet.

I knew that I wanted to build several markets and that it wouldn't be realistic to have many listings from many markets coming to my email. For our searches we do under $100,000 for foreclosures, short sales, estate sales, priced reduced, and make offer.

Offer Frequency

You now have everything you need to have your real estate agent make offers for you. Ideally you should have your agent repeat each offer once a week until there is a status change on the property. With the MLS system they can tag each property, meaning that anytime there's a change they get notified. If your real estate agent doesn't know how to do this, have them get assistance from their broker or call their MLS help line. By repeating these offers weekly you are consistently keeping a snowball of offers rolling. It also creates a feeling for the seller of the property that maybe that's all the property is worth, so they start to entertain unloading it for your low offer.

Why This Works

This system works very well for a number of reasons. Let's take a look at them.

Leverage – This system is highly leveraged! There is the saying that goes, "Either you're leveraging or you're being leveraged–you can't do both." When I heard that, it hit deep, because most of my life I had been used as the leverage. My system gives you the ability to sit in the driver's seat and leverage other people. You are using A Players as your leverage, so it's like having the best of the best at your fingertips. They will all be happy to work your system, as it benefits them as well.

Systematic – This is a system that can and should be implemented in several markets. It takes time to build up each market, but once you do it's 90% on autopilot. Then you can turn around and build up another market, and on and on. You can build up as many markets as it takes to make the income that you want to make. If you want to be a Wholesale Millionaire, then build as many markets as it takes to reach it.

Numbers – This system is based 100% on a numbers and volume approach. The more offers you make, the more deals you will get! If you want to do five deals a month then you need to make 125 offers a month. You may be able to do it all in your market, or you may need two or three markets. The point is to decide on what you need to make and build up your markets accordingly.

Cycle Proof – Every five or ten years the real estate market changes. With this system it doesn't matter. All you have to do is change the percentages of your offers. That's it! As a market drops, so do your percentages, and as a market goes up, so do your percentages.

Chapter 11: Packaging Your Deal

When it comes to investing in real estate it's all about the numbers and what story the numbers tell. So what we're going to learn in this chapter is how to put your wholesale deals together to provide your investor buyers with all the information (numbers) necessary to prove it's a good deal. The more astute your buyers are, the more they will appreciate your having packaged your deal.

Most wholesalers don't package their deals. Instead they get an offer accepted, and then they send the address and the prices they want to sell for over to their buyers by text or email. Now don't get me wrong, this can work, but it's lazy wholesaling. I want you to be lazy, but *good* lazy, as in leveraging and outsourcing, not *bad* lazy, as in not providing a thorough deal packaged with all the important info.

One reason it's so important to provide this information is that it will cut down on the time you need to sell the deal. It takes a little more time to put it together, but your real estate agent is going to be doing most of that for you. But when you have a complete package for your buyers, there's no guesswork for them. All they need to do is go through the numbers, which tells them if it's the right deal for them.

There are a few things you will need to provide the necessary information to your buyers. You will need:

- A CMA (comparable market analysis).

- Pictures.

- Rental rates from a quality property management company.

- A mortgage calculator.

- A rundown of the numbers and estimated ROI.

Let's take a look at each of these and see what they mean as well as how we put them all together to package a deal.

CMA

As mentioned above, a CMA means a comparable market analysis. Your real estate agent will put these together for you. A CMA tells us what other houses have sold for in the neighborhood of your property. This CMA is probably the most important piece to the puzzle. The CMA will have the following pertinent information that your buyer will need to analyze each deal.

Comparable properties and sale price

By providing your buyer with the other sold properties, it will give them an idea of what the market in that target area is doing along with what they should expect out of the property should they buy it. The only comparables that matter are sold's.

Occasionally an agent will add in a couple other properties that are pending or still listed. These don't count! Until a deal is closed and sold it cannot be used. If a home owner thinks their house is worth more than it is, they might list it at $150,000, but it might sit on the market for a year while similar properties sell for $120,000 to $130,000. Therefore the exaggerated list price of the homeowner cannot be used. Have your agent only include properties that have actually sold.

Length of time since sold

The CMA will tell your buyers with how quickly the other properties sold, how long they sat on the market, or if they are still on the market. If your deal is good and the comparable properties only sat on the market for thirty days or less before selling, then your buyers will know that they should be able to expect the same results. If the comparables are all over the board, then it will give your buyers reason to look into each comparable to see what the difference is. Have your agent keep the sold date to no more than one year age from the time of the CMA. The market is always changing, so comparing against properties that sold two years ago will not work, and in fact it may hurt you if the market has picked up.

Style of houses

In the CMA you will want to make sure you are comparing apples to apples. If your subject property is a three-bed ranch, then your comparables should not have two-story houses or Tudor style houses, for example. The style of the house will affect the sale price. Again, make sure your agent knows to only send you comparables of similar houses.

Beds/baths

I feel the square footage of the house is more important than the beds and baths, as sometimes these beds and baths get added or manipulated by the current or past owner, and if your subject property needs a rehab then these can be changed as well. However, it's still good information for your buyers and they will want to know they are comparing like properties.

Square footage

The square footage of the comparable properties must be within 15% of the subject property. Again, you need to compare apples to apples.

Distance from your property

CMAs are generally done within a mile radius from the subject property. It's even better to go within a half-mile radius, but sometimes you won't have enough comparables if you do this.

Decade of property

The year built of your comparable properties should be within reason. Try to get them within the same decade if possible. This generally isn't too hard. When the developers of the area of the subject property developed and built the land, chances are it was done within the same decade. But occasionally you will have new houses built on vacant lots and such, and you can't compare a house built in 2005 to a house built in 1955.

This seems like a lot of information, but all you need to know is what to request from your real estate agent. When you send them the email or have the conversation just give them the following:

Agent, when creating my CMAs please make sure they have the following...

- ✓ Only sold properties
- ✓ Last 90 days, possibly 120
- ✓ Same style of architecture
- ✓ Same beds and baths
- ✓ Square footage within 15%

✓ Distance from subject property within one mile, preferably half mile

✓ Year built within same decade

Pictures

There is the saying, "A picture is worth a thousand words." This holds especially true when submitting the package. When you provide your buyers with 25 pictures of the subject property, it leaves little to the imagination. I can guarantee that other wholesalers don't give this much detail in their packages. This is what separates the average speculator from the Wholesale Millionaire. Here is a list of the following pics you will need from each deal you get...

Exterior:

✓ Front exterior, two angles

✓ Street view of all directions

✓ Angle view of houses directly next door to subject property

✓ Side view of subject property

✓ Rear view of subject property, two angles

✓ Garage, all four sides and inside

✓ Driveway

✓ Backyard

✓ Deck/patio

✓ A/C unit

Interior:

✓ Living room/ entry area

✓ Bedrooms/ closets

✓ Bathroom(s)/ tub, toilet, vanity, floor, exhaust fan. Should be able to capture all in two pics.

✓ Kitchen cabinets, countertop, floor, eating space.

- ✓ Any additional rooms

- ✓ Basement living area / bedrooms

- ✓ Furnace

- ✓ Water heater

- ✓ Electrical panel

- ✓ Sump pump

- ✓ Foundation if exposed

Amenities:

- ✓ Close parks

- ✓ Tennis courts

- ✓ Pool

This should be more than enough pictures to give your buyers an idea of what condition the house is in, the layout, and an idea of what it can look like after being fixed up.

You might be thinking "Holy cow, this is a lot of work to ask out of my real estate agent," and you're right—it is! This is why you need an A Player! However if you look at the time they invest into each deal of yours, it's far better than what they spend on the average owner-occupied buyer or first time homeowner. Real estate agents often have to show these buyers dozens of houses, they go through inspections, run numbers, CMAs, etc. So they are doing all the same stuff for you, but they only have to do it on the deals you get accepted or countered that looks like a deal. The rest of the time all they are doing is making offers, which should take only minutes per offer.

So by doing this for you they are actually utilizing their time very efficiently. You just may have to help them see it that way, but chances are if you are working with an A Player then you don't have to pump them up or talk them into anything.

Rental Rates

Many of your investor buyers will be landlords, and they will want to know what the subject property can be rented for. This will help them analyze their ROI (return on investment) or cash flow (profit after all expenses). The easiest way to determine the rental rate is to have your real estate agent establish a relationship with one of the premier property management companies in town. Have your real estate agent inform the property management company that when they provide the estimated rental rates, you would also like comparables of other rentals in the area and what they are getting for rents. These management companies can whip these together very quickly. If they can't respond quickly, have your agent find a different management company.

The interest the property management company will have in this is you will forward the memorandum they put together to all your investors. This memorandum should have a cover page of the property management company providing the info! This is a free advertisement for them, and it's going directly to the email of all the investors in the area.

Make sure the property management company knows this; it will keep them motivated to keep your deals at highest priority.

I hope you are starting to see how magical this is. I also hope you are realizing just how highly leveraged it is. Everything is set up so that everyone benefits, yet it's almost all entirely free.

Mortgage Calculator

The mortgage calculator is to help you instantly calculate the numbers for your buyers. You are providing them with a package so that they don't have to think; all the numbers are laid out for them. You can go to:

http://www.mortgagecalculator.org/calculators/mortgage-payment-calculator.php

Here is a snapshot of what your printout will look like:

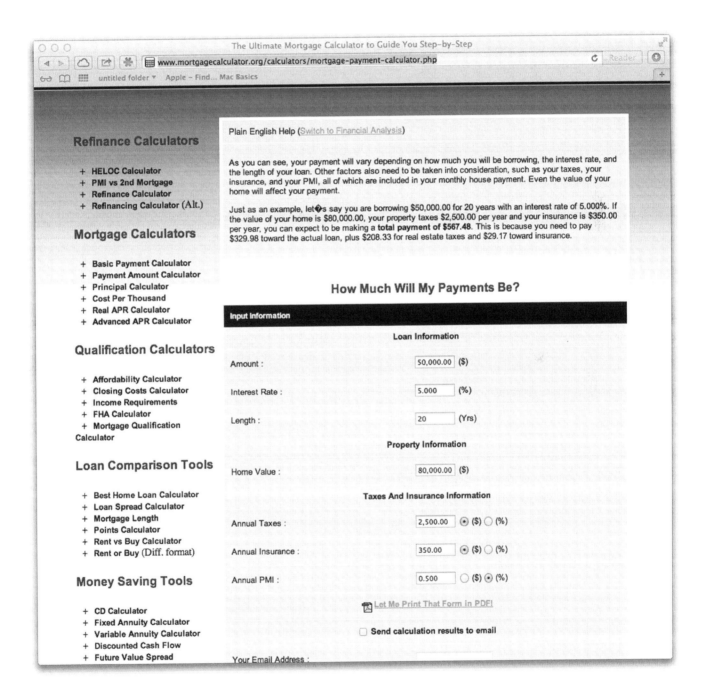

At the top of the page it spells out exactly what your investors can expect to pay. If they are a landlord, the majority of your buyers will pay cash, and then turn around and put a

mortgage on it. If they are a rehabber, this doesn't apply as much. However, if they are a rehabber and you are sending killer deals that have awesome cash flow, they might start thinking about getting into rentals.

Most banks will refinance with 20% to 30% equity. So if by your CMA the property should sell for $80,000, then the bank will likely finance between $56,000 and $64,000. The presented interest rate and term of the loan is a good rule of thumb to go by, but stay in touch with what banks are doing so you can stay ahead of the game and deliver accurate numbers to your buyers. You can make a call to any community bank and find out the current rates.

So since you have all the expenses figured out for them, all they need to do is take the expected rent rate, subtract the expenses, and they have their estimated cash flow. This does not factor in property management fees or repairs, and I have found more often than not that the average local investor does not utilize a property management company.

Deal Analyzer/ ROI

The ROI is what any astute investor should be looking at. In a nutshell it tells them how fast their money is growing–the larger the percentage, the faster it's growing. Many landlords may say they look at the cash flow, but in reality they are also looking at the ROI because that is why they want to refinance and pull their money out. This allows them to acquire an investment property, make cash flow on it every month, and possibly even pull out extra money with it if there's enough equity. This is only one strategy, but the ROI is going to be your most widely used formula for measuring investment earnings.

You can go to http://easycalculation.com/mortgage/roi-calculator.php to pull up a quick ROI calculator.

I have this example factored in for a rehabber. Let's say the rehabber bought the property from you for $60,000 and put $25,000 into the remodel, so he would have $85,000 as the initial investment. Then he sells for $125,000 - $15,000 for selling costs = $105,000 as the return amount (earnings). Hit calculate, and this rehabber should have an ROI of 23.53%. Which is extraordinary, and this is typically a three- to four-month turn around. It's actually typical in real estate, but you can't find that kind of return anywhere else. I used these numbers because this is my favorite price range to be in when I flip houses.

When submitting the ROI you don't need to forward this printout, just include estimated ROI percentage in your deal when submitting.

Submitting the Deal

Ok, so let's say you got your deal accepted. Once you get it accepted you would need to have your real estate agent do the following:

- ✓ Provide a CMA
- ✓ Take pictures
- ✓ Provide memorandum from property management company.

You should make sure your agent knows that you need these right away. I would expect them within twenty-four hours. If for whatever reason your real estate agent can't get to something, they should have someone in place who can.

Your agent should be able to send them all in the same file by email. Once you have it, you can include the mortgage calculator results as well as the ROI. Along with this you will want to include a brief synopsis as well as wording to help "sell" the property.

Let's take a look at the example property and how the email might look.

ATTENTION!!! Just in is an outstanding deal at 7606 SW 9th PL. DSM, IA. It's available for only $69,500! It only needs approximately $7,500 in repairs. Please see the following CMA showing that the ARV is $115,000.

If you flip this you can expect an outstanding profit of $28,000 and/ or an ROI of 36.6%.

According to the attached rental memorandum the property should rent for $1,025 per month. After a refinance and leaving 30% equity you are able to pull all your money out plus and additional $3,500. With taxes and insurance included it brings your payment to $743.76. This leaves you with an excellent cash flow of $281.24 per month.

Please see the attached CMA, pictures and rental memorandum to make your educated decision. This is an excellent deal. Please proceed ASAP as it's expected to move very quickly.

That's it. In those few short paragraphs you and your real estate agent gave your buyers all the information they need to make a very educated decision. Again, in the email your real estate agent would have the CMA, pictures, and rental memorandum all attached and downloadable. Within five minutes I was able to hop back and forth between these websites, do the math, and create this email. And that is exactly why this system is so great! You have to put in a little bit of leg work up front to get the system and contacts built, but after you do it literally only takes minutes to do each deal.

If you didn't notice, you just made $5,000 on this deal. Your real estate agent made the offer for you, gathered up all the most important information attached it to an email and all you had to do is spend five minutes putting the numbers together. It's insanely easy!

Closing the Deal

Closing the deal should generally run smoothly, assuming you have an A Player attorney working for you. Once you have an investor who is ready to buy your property, it's time to finalize the deal. You should have the contract between the seller and you, and you should have a contract between you (now seller) and your buyer. It does not matter if the property was listed on the MLS or if it's a homeowner who is selling, you must still have a contract on each. If it's an MLS listing, then you will be using your real estate agent's contract to buy the property, and then use the previously mentioned assignment of contract or state bar purchase agreement as the contract between you and your buyer.

If it's an off-market deal, then you can use the state bar purchase agreement for both transactions, or you can use the assignment of contract between you and your buyer. Also you will want your buyer to put up the earnest money to your attorney. I don't ever put up the earnest money or deposit. If for some reason your buyer didn't follow through, then they are the one who is out the money, not you. I have to this day never had a deal fall through due to a buyer, but I'm not going to say it'll never happen. Stay protected.

Once you have both contracts signed, you can submit to your attorney. I always scan everything to an email then submit. I also always send a copy to an email folder of that property just in case I need to resort back for something. At this point the attorney will take over and get all appropriate documentation ordered. If the attorney has any questions they will know to go to you, as this is your deal and you are their customer.

Once it's closed, have the attorney send your check by mail. If you are willing to pay extra you can ask to have it overnighted. The reason I say to have it mailed is because I want you to get in the habit of being super efficient and outsourcing. If you are going to spend the time to drive over and pick up the checks from your attorney's office, then you are spending valuable time and not making anything for it.

I have done both, but for whatever reason it's way cooler to get the checks in the mail. Maybe it's because we are used to getting bills in the mail, I don't know, but when you start getting checks in the mail of $2,500, $5,000, or $10,000, it's *awesome*!

Setting Up Your Office

The really beautiful thing about this entire system is that it can be done from anywhere in the world from the comfort of your computer and phone. The days if needing to be everywhere and at your place of business are over.

No matter where you do your business from you will need a few essentials to keep thing business running smooth and quickly.

Computer – It doesn't matter what kind as long as it has plenty of memory and is updated to be able to handle any kind of downloading, files, etc. Any computer made in the past five years or so will be sufficient. I personally made the switch to an iMac, and I love it and recommend it for you too.

High-speed internet connection – I personally don't know anyone who still has dial up, but in case you do, you need to transfer over to a high speed connection. The only reason people use dial up is to save money. Once you start doing deals, saving a few pennies will be a thing of the past.

Laser printer/fax/copy/scanner – A laser printer is much more expensive than an ink jet printer, but its capabilities far outweigh the cost. I had an ink jet for the longest time and didn't know any difference, and then one day my whole system got fried by ground lightning. Thank goodness. After that I asked around to see what my peers were using, and everyone recommended me to a laser printer. I use a Muratec MFX-c2700. They are about $1,500 and worth every penny. If need be, wait until you do a deal or two, but I advise getting one as soon as possible. The money you will save on ink alone is worth it, and they perform at such a higher speed and efficiency that the time they save will more than make up for the difference in cost.

Phone – Duh, I don't even use a landline anymore as my cell phone plan has unlimited minutes. Use a landline if you so choose, but make sure you have a cell phone so you can do business on the go.

Binders – Keep a three-ring binder of any market you are building up. In this binder you will want to keep a hard copy of your real estate agent, attorney, buyers, etc. Keep a three-hole punch along with this.

Copy paper – Always keep stocked up on copy paper. For what it costs, there is no reason to ever run out.

Note pad and pen – On your desk you should always have a notepad and pen ready for when you need to quickly jot down vital information.

That's it. You may wish to include more supplies but these are the essentials. Try to always stay organized, for some of us it's tough as we are not wired that way, but as you become more successful you will need to become more organized.

Chapter 12: Conclusion

My friend, you have just learned how to become a Wholesale Millionaire. There is a lot of detail in these pages, probably more than any other wholesaling guide out there. This system is my greatest creation to date. I didn't create this for myself–I created it for you! I'm already financially blessed and my wish is for this book and system to bless your family just as much. Let's do a recap of what you have learned, and close this with some action steps.

In the Introduction and Chapter 1, you were given a quick synopsis of the current state of our economy and how most people are going to be left behind. Our government has screwed this country in more ways than we will ever know and we are headed for a financial tidal wave of a disaster. If you are not on high ground when that tidal wave hits, you will be swept away. If you don't make a change now, how will it feel to have everything you worked so hard for to be stripped away from you in days. Mark my words, this will happen. If you have a trained eye for the economy and see its signals, you will most certainly take all-out massive action. Even worse, how will it feel to know that you had in your hands the one thing that could have saved you and your family from the devastation?

I don't write these words to scare you, but to motivate you to change your life. It's now in your hands.

We also talked about the new model of real estate. Old timers in real estate will still make their money, but it will be so much slower and harder than what you just learned to do. Leverage and systems is what propels people to legendary status. It may still take some hard work–I'm not saying all you have to do is flip a switch and you're rich. The universal laws are not set up that way. But I am telling you that with technology and systems, your real estate business of wholesaling is going to trump anything else out there.

You learned about my story from mediocrity to freedom. This can be your life. It's all in your hands. I can't say it enough–all you have to do is take massive action and your life will change before you know it. You can have anything you can imagine. As I write this, I have nine different pictures above my computer of dream houses and Lamborghinis that I plan to own. I use them as a motivator. There are other things that are far more important, but from everyone else's standards this goofy, middle-class kid with holes in his jeans shouldn't be living in a multi-million dollar house and driving a Lambo. So it's a motivator that I use to prove them wrong.

My point is that if I can do this, then you can too. There is absolutely nothing more special about me than you. In fact, in many ways you're probably smarter and more gifted than I am. One important point to understand is that you can achieve anything you desire by having a plan and taking action. I provided you with the plan; all you need to do is put it into action.

In Chapters 2 and 3, you learned about my struggles and successes. We also went through what obstacles you might be facing, and how to overcome those obstacles. This all boils down to what your reason is for doing this. The reason people stay average their entire lives is they don't have a deep enough reason to change. That's it, period.

Change is not usually enjoyable. It can be hard, uncomfortable, emotional, and exhausting. However, if we want something different, something better, then change is always necessary.

I remember a time in my life very clearly... it was four or five years ago. I had just started my journey of self-improvement and wasn't seeing the changes in my life as fast I had hoped. One afternoon I went to Barnes & Noble and purchased a Tony Robbins audio set. I anxiously drove home and popped the CDs into my CD player and grabbed a note pad. I wasn't going to be the person who listened to all the CDs but didn't do any of the exercises. Rather I did everyone of them, just as you should do with this book.

One of the exercises was to write down everything we wanted and how soon we planned to achieve them. There was supposed to be no limit to our desires, so I think I filled up a couple pages' worth. Yet, as I went to write down a time frame I couldn't really come up with anything because at that time I didn't have any direction or any purpose, and I didn't know how I would ever achieve these items I had written down.

I vividly remember sitting there, my heart pounding and my blood pressure quickly rising. Tears were streaming down my face. Finally out of nowhere I screamed out as loud as I could:

"I'M GOING TO CHANGE, I'M GOING TO CHANGE,

I WILL BE SUCCESSFUL, I WILL MAKE A DIFFERENCE!"

By screaming those words out the way I did, that conviction went cellular! I changed in an instant without really knowing how. I instantly felt liberated. It was like the little girl screaming at the big bully and he decides he doesn't want to mess with her anymore, but this time it was me against the universe. I believe the universe decided it wasn't going to win the battle, so it backed off.

Sometimes we have to let it all out. By doing this I was able to get out of my own way. Have you ever noticed how easily we get embarrassed in front of ourselves? It's crazy. It doesn't even make sense how that happens. But how are we supposed to ever become successful if we can't get out of our own way and get over ourselves? Once you can learn to get out of your own way, you will attain success at a rate you never thought possible. Just step aside and let yourself past. Just try it and see what happens.

In Chapter 4, we discovered how to build a team of A Players and their importance in your system. No matter how well put together your system is, it will not produce results if you don't have A Players on your team. They are absolutely crucial! I have had to fire many people from my business, and it's never fun, but the second you get rid of the dead weight is the second you get continue on growing.

This is because anyone who is not an A Player is wasting your time. A Players naturally take things over. It's in their genetic makeup. A Players will never say they don't have time for something. They make time. A Players will never say they can't do something. They figure out how to do it or how to get it done. The biggest reason A Players are crucial to your success is they allow you to work on your business rather than in it. Because they are efficient, it allows you to be efficient. Once you start getting bogged down with phone calls and emails from your team, you need to take a deeper look at them and evaluate.

Before pointing a finger it's always best to take responsibility. It's always easy to point the finger and blame someone else, but to be really successful takes a person who is willing to take responsibility. If you have a person on your team who is not performing, first take responsibility, and then move forward with your team. You were the one who brought that person on to your team, so it's your fault first. Correct, the problem and move forward. If at that point the teammate can't produce the way you need them to then let them go and find another.

You may get to the point where people on your team mention how loyal they have been to you, so they expect you to always take care of them. If this happens, they have a poor mindset and are not A Players. I have had everyone from real estate agents, to contractors, to lenders say this to me, and my response is always the same: loyalty and results have nothing to do with each other. When it comes to business, it's all about results. Who takes the most stress off you shoulders? Who can handle a large workload without complaining? Who is the most efficient? And who produces the most profit? The answers to these questions will determine who you need to keep and who you need to get rid of.

I have at times had to fire my real estate agents or attorneys who were very good friends of mine, but I knew that if I continued on with the same team that I would continue on with the same results.

In Chapter 5, you were given instructions on how to find a target market. I feel this is one of the coolest parts of the entire system. I don't know of any other system or course or book out there that makes it so easy to quickly scope out a market. With just a few clicks of a mouse you can find out the population of a city, its metro population, how many target properties are in the market, and the demographics of the city. If you have one or two cities you want to work in, then by all means feel free. But if you are not sure, then take some time and play around with these provided websites. It's really cool to see the differences in populations, prices of houses, and number of listings on the market.

I still find it amazing that we can so easily do business across the country from the comfort of our computer and cell phone.

I ask you for just a second to put any limitations out of your mind. What will happen if you take massive action and build up teams in several different areas? I know several people who are doing more than twenty deals per month in average size major cities. So what are the possibilities? They're endless! You can achieve whatever you can imagine possible. With this system being so virtual, and with all the houses on the market across the country, it's incomprehensible to think about all the possibilities. It's 100% a numbers game. If you only have one market you're working in and you don't have the best of the best working for you in those areas, then you can expect your deals to be limited. You will get more deals in some areas than others. In some markets you may get very little, depending on how competitive that specific market is, but the point is that you keep going. Build up as many markets as it takes to get your desired deals and income.

In Chapter 6 we discovered how to efficiently find an A Player real estate agent. As said before, you real estate agent will make or break your team, so it's crucial that you only find A Players to work with. When you find the right real estate agent they are worth more than their weight in gold. You can't put a value on them because the right one will make you so much money over and over and over again.

We also learned how to instruct your real estate agent to scope out other real estate agents in other markets for you. They should gladly screen these other agents for you, as they will get a referral fee from every deal you do with that next agent.

Be sure to reward your agent occasionally. This could be a ticket to a ball game, coffee and muffins at their office in the morning, or a steak dinner. They will be working very hard for you, so it's important for them to notice that you appreciate them.

In Chapter 7 we discovered how to find a real estate attorney or title company. The attorney or title company for your deals are also crucial parts of your team and your business because you can't do any deals if you can't close them. As discussed, we have to close a wholesale deal differently than we do a regular transaction, so it's imperative that we deal with someone who understands how these closings need to be constructed.

You were also given a sample assignment of contract and a sample power of attorney to use should you need them. The more markets I build up, the more differences I run into with what my attorneys and real estate agents need. Some real estate agents want a power of attorney to make the offers for you while others don't feel it's necessary, so it's here for your convenience should you need it.

Again, the state bar purchase agreement is the purchase agreement you will use whenever signing between you and your buyers. If there is anything you don't understand about any contract, be sure to consult with your real estate attorney.

Your Buyers Are Your Business

In wholesaling, your buyers are your customers and it's your duty to not only make sure their transaction is smooth, but also to give them exceptional service and that includes providing them with all the essential data of any deal so they are not left with any questions.

When you start approaching your wholesaling this way, you will have the ability to sell properties to people all over the country. Buyers will buy from across the country because you'll have all the numbers laid out for them and resources including the CMA, pictures, property management data and contact information, estimated ROI, and estimated cash flow. This gives your buyer total confidence in buying the deal from you. If it's a deal, then all your data shows it's a deal.

Getting back to your buyers... Your customer service to them needs to be above and beyond, just as you'd expect from any store or restaurant you step foot in. It's no different. I have bought properties from other wholesalers many times, and I can tell you that to my knowledge nobody puts together deals like you are taught to do here. You will have the advantage to blow the other wholesalers out of the water!

We also discovered how to find other wholesalers and their value to your business. Most people are ignorant when it comes to competition. I have seen many times wholesalers get jealous or bitter about new wholesalers coming into their market. These people are ignorant. Instead you should embrace other wholesalers. The more wholesalers you know, the more deals you can do and the faster you can do them. If you just found the best wholesalers in every market and networked with them you would be rich beyond measure. Why? Because they already have access to everything you need. They have their list of cash buyers, they know who does the double closes, and they know the market and what is going on. Be sure to make it a point to get to know at least a couple of good wholesalers in each market.

We also went through how to keep track of your buyers and how to make your system as automated as possible. As your business grows so will your need for efficiency and automation. Starting out, you can use notebooks and email folders to keep everything in. However, when information starts to seem scattered and you can't get things located immediately, then it means it's time to get it automated. Refer back to any of the recommended websites for creating your email list. Most of these websites are very user friendly and they have support staff who can help you out should you have any questions.

The bottom line is that you should always remember *your buyers are your business*. They are your customers–don't ever forget that. It's easy to get caught up on how much we want to make on each deal, but remember your customers, and always be mindful of the deal and make sure it works for both you and them. If you are trying to make $15,000 on a wholesale and your buyers are squeezed super tight to make it a deal, then you are not providing good service. On the flip side, you don't want to give the deal away every time and not make enough profit. Just be conscious of your buyers and you will do fine.

Become a Deal Magnet

Knowing how to find the deals will always keep you ahead of the competition, and having a system like this in place will help you smash the competition. Finding deals is what gets you paid. The mistake most seasoned investors make is that they spend a lot of time scouring listings but they wait for their real estate agent to bring them any deals. On top of that most investors don't have A Player real estate agents working for them.

Be thankful for the above scenario, as that's what is going to give you so much opportunity! If the one thing these investors lack is finding good deals and the one thing you are awesome at is finding deals, wouldn't you say there is a good chance you will be in demand? And if you are in demand, will you get paid well? Yes and yes. It's supply and demand.

Investors are generally really good at analyzing numbers, not finding great deals. The methods you learned in this book are not known by many. So assuming you take advantage of the methods and put them to work, you should never have a tough time finding deals, especially when this can be done in any city of the country. Start to think of yourself as a deal magnet. If you allow this to sink into your subconscious, you will find yourself finding more deals than you know what to do with.

Finally, you learned about the meat and potatoes of this system, which is the offering system and the spreadsheets. In any successful business there is a system of checks and balances in place to make sure things are accurate, productive, and moving forward. For us, the system of checks and balances is our spreadsheets. These spreadsheets allow us mobility by being able to check on the status of our offers at any time from anywhere. It also gives us the ability to monitor how our percentages are doing in the current market.

Without having these spreadsheets to refer to, there would be an insanely long paper trail, probably too much for any real estate agent to keep track of. But with this they can submit your offer, enter it into the spreadsheet, and move on to the next one. Before using this system I would get my real estate agent emailing me all the time with different offers that got accepted or countered, and I couldn't even remember anything about the house. I couldn't remember the address or what we offered! Now, in about thirty seconds I can see what it was listed at, what I offered, and what it got accepted or countered at.

It's not like a spreadsheet is some high tech thing, but no one else is doing this. You are going to be so far ahead of the competition it doesn't even compare. I have been on both sides of the fence. I used to be one of the investors who would scan the listings, go look at a couple of houses a week, and write up a couple of offers. What a slow way to make a living!

Now I go through the initial legwork of getting a market built, and after that I have more offers than anyone else in that market. All I do is wait for my real estate agent in that market to send me an accepted offer, and from there I put the deal package together and ship it off to my hungry list of buyers.

So, in short, these spreadsheets will save you an unbelievable amount of time. And they'll allow you to monitor everything you have going on in each market.

In the same chapter you learned how to analyze a market and how to understand if you need to increase or decrease your percentages in order to increase or decrease the number of deals you get. This method will never go out of style because it's adaptable to any market condition.

Finally, in the last chapter you learned how to put together your deal package. This will be a game changer. There is nobody out there whom I have seen who puts deal packages together for their buyers like this. This is going above and beyond what is necessary. I have sold many properties by sending a text to my buyers, but when I integrated this system and put together these packages it raised my game to whole new level. Also, by doing this you get much more respect from your buyers. Many of them might be lenders for you in the future, so if you're showing that you know how to put deals and numbers like this together, you may very well get some lending to do some larger deals.

In the last chapter you also learned how to submit your deal to your closing agent and how to do this efficiently.

Make a Commitment

If starting from scratch, one of the most important things you can do is to make a commitment of how much time you are going to invest, how many calls a day you will make, etc. The reason this is so important is because it's very easy to get sidetracked each day.

One of my other businesses I'm involved in is being a distributor for Advocare. When I began that business, many in the hierarchy stressed the importance of *making a commitment of time invested*. It's a totally personal decision of how much time to invest, and at that time I failed to do so. I would always plan out who I was going to call or how much time per week I could devote, but I never made a serious commitment of time. Go figure there would be days that turned into weeks that I would go without getting anything done. All this wasted time was a result of not having made a time commitment.

If you have a full-time job, you may only have thirty minutes a day to work your wholesaling business, but even that much can get you further than you think. You might think, "Well, I don't have the ability to quit my job and jump in full-time like you did." My answer is good, don't, it was really stressful. A half hour a day, every day, turns into fifteen hours a month, and with that amount of time invested you will get results. You just have to be *consistent* and *persistent*.

I recommend doing either or both of two plans:

1. You make a time commitment for each day. Keep it small at first, maybe only thirty minutes a day.

2. You make deadline for each piece of the system to be completed. For example, tell yourself, "I will have a real estate agent decided on by December 31. I will have my buyer's list built to twenty-five buyers by January 15."

With option two you are setting miniature goals of when you will have things accomplished. I like this route because I like setting goals, but also because if gives you flexibility. If you fall behind a day or two for whatever reason, then you will know that you need to pick things up in order to complete by the projected date.

I have this system lined out in order for the most efficient step-by-step approach. Take a moment and decide a length of time to get each part of this system built up.

Your Timeline

I will find my A Player real estate agent by _____.

I will find my real estate attorney or closing agent by _____.

I will find three other wholesalers in my market by _____.

I will build my buyers list to_____ by _____.

I will have my spreadsheets created by _____.

I will scan Craigslist for deals every _____ days.

I will have my bandit signs in effect by _____.

I want to make $_____ per month which means I need to have

_____ offers per month being made. (25:1)

I will have my first deal done by _____.

I hope for your sake that you actually went through with doing this exercise, as it has power. By doing it you are writing down your goals, which has been proven to accelerate a person's results and success.

Please do not put this book down without writing those out. Take as much time as you need, but it's crucial that you fill them out. After you are done, tear the page out or create one on the computer and print it off. Put it in your wallet or purse so you can carry it with you. Take it out and read it as often as possible. Read it out loud whenever possible. And continue to go through this book as much as you need.

Quick Story

At the beginning of this book I told about how broke I was, but I didn't go into enough detail... so here you go. Before I found real estate, I had gone through bankruptcy, been on food stamps, been in foreclosure, and had to sell many of my possessions to avoid my family becoming homeless. Much of this was my own fault, as I was never good with money, and some of this was due to job loss, layoffs, and poor decisions.

For a man who has any pride, it's a very sick feeling to not be able to provide for his family. It may be one of the worst feelings a man can experience. When I was single it was no big deal... we just don't eat as much, get another job, whatever it takes to get back to even. But the day I took on having an immediate family (my fiancée already had two kids) my income was no longer sufficient. I now had the responsibility of providing shelter and food and care for those little girls.

I remember vividly sitting at the kitchen table with my wife trying to figure out what we were going to do if we lost the house. Who wants to take in a family of four? Well, being a good man, I didn't allow us to lose the house. I worked three jobs for over a year to keep us afloat. We were able to get a loan modification, pay the late fees and keep the house... thank goodness.

Then I turned to real estate. Aside from the mortgage on our house, within eighteen months of being in real estate I was debt free. I had larger checks coming in than I had ever seen in my life. It wasn't always easy, not by a long shot. But it was a lot easier than working three jobs.

It was around this time that I actually had some good money in the bank and was feeling good about myself and my situation.

One day as I was driving around checking on some of my rehab properties, I drove by an apparently homeless man walking with no shoes on. I could tell from the wear in his socks that it had probably been a while. Something was pulling hard on my heartstrings to turn around and see what I could do. I drove through the parking lot and up to the old man who was now sitting on the curb. I waved him over to the car.

He slowly rose to his feet and wobbled over. I got right to the point and asked him what happened to his shoes. He proceeded to tell me that a few young kids jumped him the night before and stole his shoes from him. As he was telling me he began to cry. Having a seventy-year-old man break down and cry in front of you is a humbling experience. I let him finish his story and I replied by asking him if my shoes would help him. As I began taking them off he began to weep and thanked God. I am sure I could have given more but to him at that moment those shoes were his rescue.

I left there and drove for miles, weeping the whole way, and I didn't know why. I tried calling my wife to tell her about the experience, and when she answered I was silent... I was so shook up that I couldn't speak.

The moral of this story is for a change I was in a position to give! I was no longer in need. I knew that I could turn right around and go buy another pair of shoes, so the calling I had to give felt right rather than a struggle. Real estate has blessed me beyond measure and it will continue to do so, and so now it's my mission to give back to the world around me. This story may seem insignificant, but I had never felt a pureness like taking care of that man in need. Serving others is what we are put on this earth to do. The Lord says to take care of the poor, the elderly, and the sick.

Changing the World

I make no effort to hide the fact that I am a Christian man. I am proud of it and have seen countless lives changed when people turn their lives over to Christ. I'm not going to spill my faith all over these pages, but I will instead mention why I believe it's so important to make a lot of money while trying to be the best that we can possibly be.

I am sure you have noticed that our world is at war, not only in a literal aspect but in a spiritual war as well. There is too much sickness, perversion, and evil in this world–human trafficking, missing children, rape, murder, homelessness, cancer, and more. It's becoming a scary world to live in, let alone raise our children in.

But I ask you, friend, what would happen if only a small percentage of the population rose up, got uncomfortable, and changed their own lives so they could live a God-given purpose to improve the lives of others?

What would you be able to do for a better cause if you no longer had to worry about paying the bills? What if you had so much money that you had to give it away to others who needed it so much more?

Better yet, what influence would it have on your children to see their mother or father change the entire dynamics of your family because you were willing to say "yes" to getting out of your box and doing something different?

My friend, this is how we change the world! We change it by first changing our own lives so we can be a blessing to others. How are we supposed to be a blessing to others when we are broke, tired, and miserable ourselves?

You are called to be a leader. You are called to be leader in your marketplace, in your church, in your kids' schools. You are called to be a warrior and to take charge of what is in front of you! What effect do you have on anyone if you continue on doing what you are doing now? But what effect could you have on those around you if you took all-out massive action and blew this thing up?

Not only would you be in a position to bless others, but you would be a blessing to others by letting your excellence be an advocate of who you are. People will see your light shine and start asking questions. People will want a piece of what you have, and you will be in a position to educate them on how to do the same.

Our world can be changed if we just give our all in everything we do! Take that massive action, get those deals done, and make a ton of money. Don't dare quit. You are worth it. Keep going until your excellence propels you into the next chapter of your life.

You are divine. You were created by the most high God to live out a divine purpose. You have in your hands a recipe for freedom and abundance. Use it to change your life and the world around you!

God Bless.

Mark

Made in the USA
San Bernardino, CA
24 September 2014